How to Build
Your Management Skills

How to Build

McGRAW-HILL

Your Management Skills

Joseph G. Mason

BOOK COMPANY

New York
San Francisco
Toronto
London
Sydney

HOW TO BUILD YOUR MANAGEMENT SKILLS

07-040686-3
First McGraw-Hill Paperback Edition, 1971
5678910 MUMU 7

To my wife, Ann, and my children,
Judy and David, all of whom cooperated
beautifully while this book was being written.

Preface

The subject of management is broad and complex. The types of personalities found in the ranks of the managers are equally varied. Anyone attempting a book on the practice of management must, therefore, make a decision as to which of two basic approaches he will take:

He can limit his discussion to a specific level of management such as *policymaking, middle management, first line supervision,* etc. Or, he can assume that there are certain areas of commonness in managing, and deal with these. The "commonness" approach is the one used in this book.

The author believes that *managing* is *managing;* that it is active, not passive. And it doesn't make any difference to the manager what his level is at the time he has to manage. Whether he is acting in the capacity of the president of a major automobile company, as a general manager of a division of a large food processor, as a buyer in a department of a retail store, or as the head of the house in a strictly family situation, the manager is the one in charge at the moment—he is the one who has to analyze the journey, plot the course, point out the starting direction, get the bodies in motion, and then accept responsibility for the outcome of the venture.

This author also believes that there are instances of just as good management being applied to the conduct of a neighborhood P.T.A. group as those applied in many major corporations; and that there are many examples of businesses as poorly managed as are some unincorporated township street and road departments.

In this book, therefore, you will find such terms as *manager, executive, supervisor,* etc., used almost interchangeably. From the context, however, you should be able to place the specific level of authority being referred to wherever this is important to the discussion.

This, then, is a book for managers in the sense of "those who manage"—the men who are the practical practitioners in business, government, and society in general. In other words, for those who actually keep the wheels turning by making things happen—no matter what their actual titles.

Joseph G. Mason

Acknowledgments

The author wishes to thank both *Nation's Business* and *Business Management* magazines for their generous permission to adapt material which originally appeared in those publications to the needs of this book.

J.G.M.

Contents

1

Introduction: The Manager and His Job

One of the most used but seldom defined words in business is "management"—often spelled with a capital *M*. But studying its usage, you begin to wonder if anyone has really agreed on what it means. And until we agree on what management means, we cannot really reach agreement on who a manager is.

Consider for a moment the question: Who is management in your company? Is the president management? Chances are you will agree that he is. Is a foreman management? Some people include foremen in the term—at least most unions promptly exclude them from membership as soon as they get to be foremen. But if you define both the president and a foreman as management, what is their common bond?

One widely accepted definition of management states that it must include policy-making authority. According to this theory, a foreman is left out and so is the entire group of people popularly termed "middle management." But in many situations a good foreman will make more policy-type decisions in a day than his mahogany row superior will in a month. Not always as big, or as critical, or as costly, of course, but relatively just as important within the sphere of his operations as the president's are within his sphere.

Another definition of management is: "It's a verb, not a noun." This is getting closer to reality. It includes everyone who makes something constructive happen in the business of the company. It includes the president, middle-level executives, foremen, the individual salesman in the field, and the correspondence clerk in the order department. But perhaps this definition is too all-inclusive. Among other things, if everyone were in management, it would destroy the reason for status and stature, and would probably discourage the bright young men just out of college.

So in this book we will use a third definition of management, possibly not the best, but still one that has the element of practicality to it: Management is the act of accomplishing events through other people. And this brings us to the working definition we are really after: A manager is one who accomplishes events through other people.

It is possible, of course, to look on management as an art. But this may seem rather "blue sky" to some otherwise hardheaded executives. However, successful managers are creative in their approaches to managing. But creative with a continuing regard for the practical, in that they approach the job of managing, or leadership, as a fluid activity—one that must be handled in an imaginative, personal way. No real manager would ever attempt to formalize his managing into set routines based on predictable actions and reactions. As Professor Emery Stoops of the University of Southern California puts it: "Leadership is complicated. It is intellectual; it is emotional; and it is physical. It is inherited and it is learned. It is the summation of the total man which must square with myriad desires of the group."

And this, naturally, brings the problem of acquiring the personal skills to make yourself a better manager squarely into perspective: there are no formulas, no easy rules, no quick answers to becoming a better manager. Every manager or potential manager or would-be manager must start with what he has: himself. And he must build on that as well as he is able. And he must do it himself. A company can give any man the title of "manager," but only the man can make himself into one.

The characteristics required to manage are a different matter. These we can generalize on to some extent. And we can also say that whether a man is a good manager or a bad manager will depend entirely on how well he personally brings the following characteristics to bear within the framework of his job:

The essence of managing is to take risks, to make decisions. Sometimes, of course, the manager manages best by delaying a decision, or even by refusing to make one. But this still entails a risk, because delay may give a problem a chance to grow. It is a fundamental of managing that the person who is not willing to take the risk of deciding will never be a manager.

The challenge of the manager is people. This complicates his job. It means that he must know people in general and his own people in particular. He must understand people and their capabilities, weaknesses, aptitudes, drives, and motivations. It does not, contrary to some popular thought, mean he must like people. But he must understand them. And he must acquire certain skills in working with them.

The technique of the manager is to work through his people. This of course adds to his risks. When he delegates responsibility, he must delegate authority with it. This means the manager is gambling on the people to whom he must give authority. And that is really his biggest and often most difficult challenge: to give people the freedom to use authority without restriction and with full support for the outcome of any actions they take.

The measure of the manager is results; there is no other. Results, of course, are a total thing: getting a job done is one thing; getting it done efficiently is another; getting it done at a profit is still another. And getting the job done in such a way that the people who do it don't all resign on you is still something else. But the only way to measure a manager is by the results he obtains.

The creed of the manager must be courage. Or, as has been said, "If you would claim the credit, be ready to accept the blame." The buck stops at the real manager's desk. He does not try to pass it upwards; he never tries to pass it down to subordinates. This means the manager must, above all else, be a *man*. He must be willing to stick his neck out and take a chance. He must be willing to fight for what he really believes is right. He must be willing to back his people when they are right. "If you would claim the credit, be ready to accept the blame." No man can be a real manager—no matter what his title—if he doesn't believe and practice this.

As you may have guessed by now, we are not setting up the manager's job as an easy one. The characteristics are there as performance needs; they can be found in the lives of all successful managers in relatively high degrees. And while there are no pat formulas for how any individual manager can live up to these qualities, there are certain generalized areas where experience would indicate he should make himself skillful:

The manager must know himself in order to be able to maximize his own capabilities—to make the most of his strengths and to develop methods to compensate for his weaker qualities.

He must understand the role his company expects him to play, because this is the framework that bounds his authority and the field he is expected to fill with his performance.

Today's manager will have a tremendous respect for facts, and a driving desire to obtain the information to reduce the so-called intangibles of business to specific factors that he can weigh and apply intelligently to his problems and his decisions.

He must understand innovation. Even though he may not be a highly creative person himself, he must be able to encourage and direct the creativity of others. It is only through innovation that a company can continue to grow and progress.

In this same vein, he will also understand ideas—those nebulous and relative contributions that individual efforts make to the success of the whole.

The manager must be apt at delegation. There has been a great deal written and said about this topic by a great many people. But it all nets down to one realistic fact: there is always some absolute limit to the amount of work even the most willing person can do. Once that limit is passed, if a man or an organization wants to continue to grow and prosper, there must be a division of labor—the work must be spread around. And someone must hand off some of the work he has been responsible for to others. He must delegate.

At the same time, the manager himself must be able to accept responsibilities that are delegated to him. If he is fortunate, he probably learned this before he reached executive or management ranks. But the newly arrived manager is often surprised or even dismayed on finding out that the responsibilities delegated to him are far more frightening in their implications and scope than those he had been used to receiving.

The successful manager will usually be a master at utilizing time—his own time, and the time of his subordinates. Time is a tool—along with money, manpower, and resources. But time is the one tool that cannot be replaced if it is wasted. The good manager will not, therefore, let it be squandered or dissipated.

The manager must also be adept at motivating others to want to solve problems. And his motivation must be of a high enough level to cause others to want to do their best— rather than just to do the job.

And, of course, since the manager's prime purpose in being is to make decisions, he must know the essentials of arriving at sound decisions. This also includes the knowledge of when to stick by a decision which has been made, as well as when to reverse a decision that is proving out to have been a bad one.

Finally, the manager must take a personal, subjective view of all of this. Managing must be a way of life. It cannot be mastered as an academic exercise. A book such as this, or an instructor in a management development course, or a college professor, or a well-intentioned superior can only give guidance by pointing out directions and making available the experience of others from which principles are derived. But only the man can make himself skilled in the art of practical managing.

A further complication for the man who wants to improve his managing is that, even as you are reading this, the job of managing is changing. The managerial art is becoming more complicated. The problems of the manager are becoming more complex. And the tools and techniques are multiplying in almost unbelievable profusion. One effect of all this is that yesterday's knowledge can often seem to be the most obsolete factor in an executive's life.

It used to be, even relatively recently, that an executive with ten or fifteen years' experience with a company was able to permit himself, every now and then, the luxury of feeling that perhaps he had "arrived," so far as being on top of his job was concerned. But today he can never be sure. In the past, an executive was expected to make his fair share of decisions and, if lucky, a fair share of those turned out right enough to get him by. He could with some certainty predict competitive countermoves to anything his company planned to do. And, chances are, he knew his company's products from raw materials to final paint coat.

But suddenly everything seems to have changed. The decisions he wants to make on hunch aren't accepted. Bright young men with masters' degrees want to know not only what he wants to do, but also exactly to what extent, and how long he expects to prolong the action. In advance. With numbers.

Competitors who used to take six months to react to a change in marketing strategy now, thanks to their own bright young men, start the battle in six weeks—or less.

As for the product, it now has so many new materials and mysterious components in it that our man is afraid to touch it when he walks through the plant.

And his big problem is still to be faced: can he renew himself fast enough to stay on top of the changes in his changing job? Will he have the ambition, the dedication, the courage, and the drive to give up what has probably come to be a comfortable way of middle-age executive living and get back to "hitting the books," as he did when he was younger and first starting up the executive ladder?

The new management concepts stemming from computer applications and the new product technologies pouring out of the laboratories are changing the job of the executive and manager on a continual and continuing basis. And the changes are just beginning now. Where they will end is anybody's guess. But the future is always different from the present—and it always arrives before you think it will. Chances are, one day soon, the personnel selection people will add a new category to the preferred characteristics for an executive: a continuing capacity to renew.

How any individual reacts to this challenge of the need for continuing renewal will depend to a great extent on his past experiences in learning. As the policy booklet of the

U.S. Army Management School states: "Learning about management and leadership is quite different from their practice. Memorizing a list of Do's and Don'ts does not necessarily improve a manager's effectiveness or behavior in getting things done through and with his personnel and organization... *unless*... the manager develops a constructive attitude toward himself and the personnel with whom he works... [and unless] he studies his own motives and behavior along with their effect upon all concerned... [and unless] he is receptive to new ideas and continuously fosters innovation for better ways to do things."

Which brings us, at long-winded last, to the purpose of this book. It was not the author's intent to provide pat answers or formulas someone could follow to become a better manager. This would be too presumptuous because, as already stated, these just don't exist. You will, however, find in this book a distillation of principles that have made other managers successful, with many examples of how the principles were applied in practice. It is up to you, however, to use your own imagination and experience to relate these to your own company, your own problems, your own people, and yourself.

Hopefully, you will also relate them to some specific goals —for without goals, all other personal efforts are meaningless. If you have never given much thought to what you, as a manager or potential manager, should have as goals, you are most sincerely invited to consider these:

We must build a sense of excellence in everyone with whom we have contact, not only subordinates and workers, but also family, friends, and the nation at large. This is accomplished through stimulating people's imaginations with insights to things as they could be rather than as they are.

We must give people a sense of confidence—in themselves and in their own abilities to cope with new and strange conditions and new situations in a continually changing world. This is accomplished by giving others the opportunities for successful realization of their own innate creativeness.

We must, of course, pass on the accumulated knowledge of the past. After all, "the man who ignores the mistakes in history is condemned to repeat them." But at the same time, we must also develop human beings who can absorb what is already known and apply it to the myriad problems of living in a constantly changing world.

We must encourage our identifiable creative minds to extend themselves to pioneer beyond the frontiers of existing knowledge so that we may increase the general store of knowledge.

And we must, above all, encourage others to use their imaginations actively so that they do not merely multiply the types of adults so prevalent today: those who are so intent on preventing small errors that they block big progress.

2

The manager must understand the role his company expects him to play because this is the framework that bounds his authority and the field he is expected to fill with his performance.

Know the Role You Are Expected to Play

It was William Shakespeare who said, "All the world's a stage, and all the men and women merely players."

This observation is now beginning to get some serious psychological investigation, particularly as it applies to business executives and other supervisory-level workers. Both clinical and industrial psychologists are now conducting investigations into what they term the "role theory" of executive behavior.

Briefly, the role theory can be summed up as the belief that a man's performance does not depend on what he really has in the way of ability, knowledge, imagination, or general capabilities, but what he thinks he has. The preliminary work that has been done in this leads some exponents to believe that an understanding of the effects of "role playing" in the executive world may have far-reaching effects, not only in improving executive efficiency, but also in such prime areas as business organization, executive selection, training, and responsibility assignments.

Everyone, of course, has his own idea of what an executive should be. Any description would probably include such qualities as leadership, initiative, dependability, judgment, getting along with people, ambition, and so forth. But these, of course, are words of imprecise definition, even by management authorities. They do not show the subtle inner- and inter-relationships that exist in a company and that, in many cases, are the actual means of carrying on the work of the company. Also, any individual stamps the role he plays with his own personality, and this alone is enough to make a formal organization chart a mere reflection of what someone would like to think his organization is like. Furthermore, any evaluation of the performance of an executive can, at best, be only a reflection of what someone else thinks the man is doing, rather than a true picture of his actual efficiency. Finally, in attempting self-evaluation, it is a rare individual who will concede that he himself does not display most of the "desirable" executive characteristics.

Before examining the role theory as applied to executive behavior, it is necessary to define "role" as we will use it here. The role represents a position, responsibility, or status, either real or imagined, within a company. This role we assume to have certain rights and duties that go with it—the expectations we have of an executive with a given job assignment. Such roles are, of course, established by the organization, or individuals in it, to carry out the organization's purpose in life. When an executive satisfactorily plays his role, and all other executives and workers are likewise playing their roles, the organization operates at peak efficiency and effectiveness. However, any organization—social as well as business—is made up of real people, each of whom has his own strengths and limitations.

Generally, the factors that will affect how an individual performs his assigned role can be grouped as follows:

The task he must do, and his understanding of it.

A situation he must be concerned about.

An attitude he feels he must maintain.

What the position means to his personal life.

His expectations for the future.

We will examine these through the use of hypothetical case studies of executives playing the roles their companies have assigned them:

Case No. 1: The Task Role and Harold Green

Green has just been appointed marketing director for his company, following a successful seven years as sales manager. His appointment came as a result of a general company reorganization aimed at consolidating certain operations in complementary, but not similar, product lines. Green has been told that his new position will include management of product planning, market research, distribution activities, advertising, and the sales department. He has not been told how to do this; he has been told only that he is to meet the general objective of "developing a good tight operation."

Green is delighted with his new assignment. For one thing, he conceives of it as an opportunity to take care of all his former complaints about products, distribution policies, advertising, and lack of management support for the sales force. He believes, with some justification, that the company's salesmen are the ones who provide the salaries for all other employees, the profits for management, and the dividends for stockholders. He, in short, sees himself as a sort of super sales manager with all the power and prerogatives he has been wanting for some time in order to save the company from itself.

Diagnosis: Green is bound to fail in his new position. Any company is an institution with a purpose. Company policies and internal structures are established to carry out certain ends. These ends serve as the criteria against which any practices or individual role performances must ultimately be measured. The reason Green will fail in the job is that his ends are not those of his company. His understanding of the role he is to play is not the role that was written for him when management decided to restructure the organization in order to get both tighter control and increased flexibility into their marketing functions. The company conceives of the marketing director's role as that of coordinator and administrator. Green conceives of it as a glorified specialist. The role conflict is clear cut. Green will lose. Perhaps the company will also.

Treatment: In making a new responsibility assignment, it is sometimes difficult to discern the degree of understanding that a man has of his new role at the time the assignment is made. In the case of Harold Green, the understanding did not, obviously, exist. This may have been due to Green's own preconceived notions of what it would take to strengthen the company's selling operations—which is all he considered marketing to be—or it may have been the failure of management to give him a proper orientation and indoctrination into what they saw his new position as being.

Any change from a familiar role to a new role in a company calls for a management analysis of the position, a study of the capabilities of the man who is going to fill that position, and a proper indoctrination of the man to bridge the gap between the expectations and the realities. And until the man is known to be filling his new role to the complete satisfaction of both management and himself, he must have supervision aimed at adapting him to the role.

Case No. 2: The Situation Role and Jim White

White has been president of his company for the last two years. He came to that job from the position of vice-president in charge of the company's financial and legal affairs. His approach to the presidency was well-organized, detailed, and thorough. He has, in short, "gone by the book." Until about seven months ago, White was strictly in the driver's seat. And the company was doing well. But recently there have been signs of labor unrest. Though wage scales are protected by contracts for another eight months, the number of grievances filed by the union is almost double the rate of a year ago. His middle-management group is becoming uneasy also. Three of what White had always considered his most reliable men have left the company for other jobs, and he knows with certainty that one of his key division managers is looking around. White has continued to play the role he envisions for the company president: the man in command—remote and aloof from the day-to-day troubles that are occurring; insistent that policies and operational standards be strictly met; reserving to himself the final decisions on any matters of enough importance to be reported on the company's balance sheet.

Diagnosis: White is in trouble; so is his company. In playing out the role he has assigned to himself, and which, admittedly, has worked successfully for enough time to confirm his belief that it is the right role, he has overlooked two prime principles of managing a situation that is in a state of change: flexibility and the human element. His adherence to the strict captain-of-the-ship attitude does not take into account either the changes that are going on in the market for executive talent, which makes it easier for really ambitious men to find new jobs, or the social changes that have changed, in their turn, the base from which labor lives, works, and bargains today. His ignorance of the human element in managing has caused his better executives to become frustrated and disillusioned about their own futures as his assistants. This, in turn, has communicated an uneasiness down to the worker levels.

Treatment: It is doubtful that there is a treatment that can be made to work for Jim White. His corrections can only come from within himself, and as long as he continues to hold aloof from friendly suggestions by others, his troubles can only get deeper. White's counterparts, however, are frequently found in younger executives or supervisors of smaller groups in any company. For these men, with proper guidance and education, there is hope of either eliminating their unfortunate attitudes, or at least of mitigating them to the point where they will not harm the company as they manage in their assigned roles. Such men must learn that every single business decision has its human elements; that, as long as a company is dependent upon workers to carry out their assignments, every person in the role of supervising assignments must be a human relations practitioner. No executive can get by with merely an expert knowledge of books, or accounting, or mechanical processes, or successful sales gimmicks. He must also understand people and how to work with them—their interests, motivations, and idiosyncrasies. And finally, an executive must learn to delegate or cease to grow himself. If he insists on reserving all decisions to himself, he is neglecting the human need for growth and self-satisfaction—he is preventing his subordinates from realizing their own capabilities and frustrating them from achieving their own feelings of accomplishment that come through the successful completion of difficult tasks.

Case No. 3: The Attitude Role and Albert Brown

Brown was a man on a spot and he knew it. As executive vice-president of a small company that had been bought out by one of the giants of its industry, he was threatened with not only a loss of position and power, but also the possibility of direct financial loss. The necessary merger of his former company's personnel into the new parent company left him on a much lower level in the organizational structure. Brown, however, had true executive understanding and ability. He realized that his future in the larger company would depend entirely on how well he could integrate himself into the new organization. Furthermore, he felt that the responsibility was his to prove himself at any job assigned to him, and he had no feelings that the new company was obliged to find a berth for him merely because they had needed the physical and engineering assets of his former company. In his new and temporary assignment as assistant production manager for the larger company, Brown decided to capitalize on his assets: imagination and a sense of organization. He firmly resolved that he would not let himself become frustrated or embittered because much of the administrative detail that went with his new job really was below both his experience and his capabilities. And though he frequently did not feel like it, he did a convincing job of playing the role of a friendly, cheerful, and self-confident executive who was always ready to lend a helping hand anywhere in the division his talents might be useful.

Because the role of supervisor and subordinate cannot really be defined except in relationship to one another, Brown's attitude soon brought him to the attention of top management. People react to one another mainly by imitation, and it was soon noticed that the general level of performance in the production part of the company was improving to the extent that costs were dropping more than just "routine" efficiency could account for. When management began to analyze the changes, they found that most of the improvements and innovations, while not always directly traceable to Albert Brown, nevertheless seemed to be centered around him and the people he had direct contact with. The symptoms were strong enough, in fact, that Brown was soon promoted to full manager status, and his future in the company was secured.

Analysis: Just how far up a man can go in the business

world is dependent upon his own analysis of his abilities. If he can make a true analysis, and plan his performance role to maximize his own personal assets and subordinate his liabilities, he can make himself felt in not-to-be-ignored ways. The danger, of course, is that a man may make a wrong analysis of his own abilities. If he cannot then be brought to realize his true strengths and weaknesses, either in personal evaluation sessions, or through exposure to executive development programs, he will fail to live up to the role he has assigned himself or the one the company has assigned him on the basis of his self-claimed abilities. Since it is an obligation of the leader not to go by "the book," but rather to write the book, Brown was successful because of his true analysis of his own position and the active and noticeable demonstration of his leadership abilities.

Case No. 4: The Personal Position and Tom Black

Black served as an engineering group supervisor for about three months, although management had not made his new position official. Tom's qualifications for the position seemed good: he was a successful development engineer with several unique and profitable patents to his credit. He had always been a quick study when it came to acquiring any special technical knowledge, and, although he was somewhat lacking in an understanding of people and what is required to supervise them, his immediate superiors assumed that he could pick up any needed knowledge for this also. Black was quite happy with his prospects at first. For one thing, once his promotion became official, it would mean more money for him. And his wife was pleased at the prospect of having a husband who carried executive status. In the small community in which Black's company was located, company status and community status were almost one and the same thing.

Both Black and his wife felt this new position called for changes in both their ways and standards of living. And they began in small ways to live up to the roles they felt they were now called upon to play. Unfortunately, neither Black nor Mrs. Black were well-suited to the role of social leaders. Having always lived quiet and rather introspective lives, the change to what they felt was a necessary out-going attitude proved to be somewhat beyond them. Their happiness in the new position was short-lived. Black's work began to suffer. Rather than acquiring the knowledge management expected him to pick up, he went in the opposite direction—he became supercritical, withdrawn, and noncommunicative at times when he should have been ready to coach or assist his section members. When his division manager called him in for a talk, to help point out some of his shortcomings, it had just the opposite effect from what was desired. Black turned stubborn, resentful. And the management decision was reluctantly made to transfer him back to development work and groom a new supervisor for the position. Whereupon Black resigned from the company.

Diagnosis: Black's problem was one of confused identities. He and his wife mixed his new responsibilities and obligations on the job with what they thought the position would have to mean in his personal life. He probably could have accommodated the minor personal and personality adjustments he would have to make on the job, but in combination with the assumed social pressures, the changes were just too much for him to handle. Whenever a role incumbent is required to conform simultaneously to a number of expectations, whether real or imagined, which are contradictory or inconsistent with his role handling abilities, the expected and the actual roles conflict. This usually, as in the case of Black, results in keeping the individual at odds with his organization because he cannot stabilize his concept of the role that he must play. Black's resignation under the circumstances should not have surprised his management. Once a man has the prestige of supervisory stature, he is not likely to welcome the idea of being demoted again to "just another engineer"—even though he'd be both happier and more productive in that role. In our culture, the social pressures for status and prestige are too strong.

Treatment: The best cures for the Black type of situation are all in the nature of preventives. First the practice of temporary promotions must be used with discretion—and only upon careful analysis of the man to make sure he will not lose his perspective during the temporary phase of his assignment. Some types of individuals respond to the challenge of this kind of opportunity. Others, like Black, get out of step in their role and suffer defeat. Next, the practice of promoting a good craftsman—be he engineer, salesman, art director, accountant, or shipping clerk—on the basis of his demonstrated capabilities at his present job is fraught with dangers. Because a man is a good engineer, capable of original and creative thinking, does not automatically qualify him for a supervisory position. Your star salesman, on the basis of his personal selling abilities alone, is not qualified per se to be a sales manager. Other abilities are called for in the executive ranks, and the man should have them, or he should be given opportunity and encouragement to develop them, before being promoted to where he will have to start using such abilities from the first day on.

Case No. 5: The Future Expectations Role and John Gray

Gray is a machinist in the metal-working shop of his company. He is ambitious, personable, does his work well. His foreman recommended that he be considered for the next foreman's opening that occurred. On the basis of this, the department manager decided to interview Gray so he could "look him over firsthand." Gray proved to be satisfactory in every sense but one: a rather independent attitude toward the company itself. He seemed to feel that as long as he did his job well, and his performance and behavior remained above average, that this was as much as the company had a right to expect of him. He was not, in short, an organization man. When asked if he thought he could suitably represent management as a foreman dealing with the union members under him, Gray's reply was, "That depends on whether or not I think management is in the right." The department manager put a hold on the recommendation that Gray be made a foreman. This did not rule out the possibility that Gray could ever become a foreman. It just delayed it.

Analysis: The department manager was probably right. Gray at this time was not ready to assume the management role of foreman as his company considered it. While it is true that no man should be expected to idolize a company to the extent of completely ignoring his own intelligence, judgment, and knowledge of human nature, the roles which are required in managing any business must be established with the goals of the business in mind. In the case of Gray's company, one of the demands made on foremen is that they represent management. This is the role of any foreman in that company. By his own admission, then, Gray was not ready to play this role.

Treatment: Since Gray had demonstrated other qualities that would help make him a good foreman and future management material, the best treatment is probably to try to help him broaden his viewpoint. For example, he might be asked to sit in on foremen's meetings; participate in grievance processing; take special training or development courses—all aimed at giving him a better understanding of the management side of business. The company itself should demonstrate and communicate a special interest in him to try to build a feeling of loyalty and identification with company goals.

To sum up the necessity of knowing the role you are expected to play, we can say that every business or other type organization was organized and is assumed to be operating for a specific purpose. This means there must be goals and expectations that will result in the proper conduct of the business. When both the goals and the purposes are known and the methods to achieve those ends are also known and understood, the various means to the ends can be organized into roles.

Such roles are frequently set up before the individuals to fill them have been determined. The person finally selected for a given job or position may or may not have the initial skills needed to fit the role expected of him exactly. Nevertheless, the role must serve as the norm for the behavior of the person filling it. How much departure from this norm management is willing to tolerate will usually depend on whether such departures have constructive or destructive results.

A man cannot be considered to be satisfactorily filling his company-assigned role unless he is adjusted to it to the extent that he is performing up to all the expectations for the role. However, he must be integrated into the role to the extent that he is also satisfying his own needs and urges for self-realization. Any job is more than just what a man does for income. And if the personal satisfaction does not go along with the effectiveness of the performance, neither the man nor the company can stabilize their relationships.

*The manager himself must be able to accept
responsibilities that are delegated to him.
But the newly arrived manager is often surprised and even dismayed on finding out
that the responsibilities delegated to him are
far more frightening in their implications
and scope than those he had been used to receiving.*

3

Take Charge of Your
Own Responsibilities

Much has been said in business manuals, self-help articles, and management development clinics about the executive's responsibility to delegate responsibilities. The art of *accepting* responsibilities, however, has not been nearly so well covered. But every executive, up to and including the chairman of the board, does have responsibilities which he must accept and carry out. And the ability to handle such responsibilities effectively and efficiently is one of the key measures of any executive.

Unfortunately, in this area the usual guides developed by psychologists and aptitude testers do not offer much help in spotting a man with the potential to handle responsibility. Nor do they offer many guides to the man who is seeking to improve his own capacity to handle responsibility. Tests in use today are considered reasonably reliable for jobs where aptitude and intelligence are the main considerations. But when it comes to the intangibles of motivation and drive, both major factors in any individual's capacity to take responsibility, the tests fall down. Furthermore, the tests cannot really distinguish between the natural abilities a man was born with and the acquired abilities he has picked up in the course of his experience. As W. W. Culp, now president of the Ohio College of Applied Science, and former commandant of the U.S. Army Management School, says: "Leaders and managers are *made:* admittedly some are *born* with better equipment than others."

Therefore, the most reliable guides we have today are empirical in nature—they are based on what we can learn from observation and analysis of men who seem to be outstanding in their abilities to accept, absorb, and execute responsibilities.

As a first generalization, we can say that a man who can successfully and cheerfully accept and carry out responsibilities is one whose breadth of understanding gives him a mature approach to his superiors, his own job, his subordinates, problems of the business, and the future. And any individual's effectiveness in carrying out responsibilities will depend upon the degree of interaction of these elements within his personality.

Understanding superiors: Most jobs entailing continuous or regular acceptance of responsibilities are of a supervisory nature. They require making things happen and getting things done, usually through other people. The supervisor's prime responsibility, however, is to achieve goals set by his management. There is nothing wrong, bad, inhuman, or immoral in his striving to carry out management's goals— that is what he is there for; that is the role he is expected to play.

According to Edward J. Green of Westinghouse Air Brake Company, "Good management requires the effective application of resources to accomplish optimum objectives. This means that the manager must understand his objectives so thoroughly that he can determine which are the most important. And then he must make sure that he mobilizes the right resources at the right place at the right time in the right way to accomplish those objectives."

If you are a supervisory executive, then you must consider yourself one of your management's basic resources. This requires that you have a basic understanding of management itself—what it is, what it is for, and how it operates.

Essentially, the main task of management is to get the best out of the men and women on the payroll to accomplish predetermined goals which will, hopefully, advance the cause of the business. This means that your superiors—management—must first get a group of human beings interested in a task, and then motivate them to want to accomplish that task. You, then, are management's aid in accomplishing this. The late C. Wright Mills explained this position of the supervisory executive in his book, *White Collar; the American Middle Classes,* this way:

"You carry authority, but are not its source.... Your authority is confined strictly within a prescribed orbit of occupational actions, and such power as you wield is a borrowed thing.... You are the servant of decision, the assistant of authority, the minion of management. You are closer to management than the wage-workers are, but yours is seldom the last decision."

The supervisor, even while seeking to carry out management goals, also has a secondary responsibility to the work group of which he is a member. Furthermore, his own management, which needs him to get things done, frequently obstructs, restricts, and channelizes him in the exercise of his job. He is, in fact, often hampered by the attitudes and behavior of the very superiors he must serve.

But your prime responsibility as an executive is always

upwards—to your management. And this involves a prime responsibility to keep management informed also. Any person committed to carry out an assigned responsibility should make it a rule never to let his boss be taken by surprise by anything that has happened or is about to happen in connection with his work. Since a management superior cannot fully pass on all the responsibility for the successful completion of a job or activity, he needs to know at all times what is going on. He should be kept informed as to progress, or the lack of it, on any specific plans, projects, or programs. If everything is going well, that very fact will free his mind for more important matters. If there is trouble, or a mistake, or some other form of setback, the sooner management knows about it, the better they will be able to help avert disaster, or at least to minimize the damage. After all, a mistake promptly recognized can often be rectified before it has done any great amount of harm. Therefore, it is a prime responsibility that you keep your superiors informed of how you are executing the responsibilities they delegate to you.

Job knowledge: Nothing attracts confidence and respect for a man more quickly, both from superiors and subordinates, than demonstrated knowledge. This includes acquired information relative to a task, an understanding of the job and its duties, and the appreciation of capabilities among various subordinates. Furthermore, the man who knows his job builds confidence in himself as well as in others. At the same time, lack of knowledge cannot be concealed, at least for long. While it is sometimes possible to bluff to gain a temporary advantage if there is something you do not know, it is usually better in the long run to admit it, along with a statement of intent to get the information.

Sources of job information are usually readily available: training programs, company literature, job specifications, operating manuals. Also industry papers and reports covering conventions, conferences, and institutes of various types. And, of course, trade, business, and general news publications for the broad, general background against which all business is conducted. It is also important, of course, that you utilize the information you acquire.

Whenever you are tempted to go to your boss with a problem, or to ask for instructions or advice, first think the situation through to the point where you have your own solution to suggest. Better still, be able to suggest alternative solutions. The human mind, even an ambitious one, is apt to be lazy at times. When it works out one solution to a problem, it is tempted to slip into neutral. That particular problem is solved. But the best that can be said, ordinarily, is that one solution has been found. It is not necessarily the best solution, or even the right one.

So consider the advice and suggestions of your own subordinates before making any recommendations to higher management. No two people think in exactly the same way, and your subordinates may furnish valuable insights and ideas that have not occurred to you in determining a problem solution.

Michael Faraday, the nineteenth century scientific pioneer, could have been advising a modern business executive when he said, "The philosopher should be a man willing to listen to every suggestion, but determined to judge for himself. He should not be biased by appearances; have no favorite hypothesis; be of no school; and in doctrine have no master."

So far as time and circumstance permit, try to plan for every possible contingency in a problem solution. It should be a sobering thought that the idea or approach you neglect in your planning may be the one that your competitor will exploit. And if he does, how will you react?

Demonstrate, as often as you can, that you are ready and willing to accept responsibilities. If you know what problems your immediate superior is struggling with, or if you can find out what they are, try to work out solutions on your own. Try to volunteer information and suggestions in the form of tentative solutions for consideration. One caution worth observing, particularly if you are tendering advice which a superior did not ask for, is to make sure your suggestions hold water. No matter how ingenious or imaginative your solution may be, always take a final look at any problem solution and ask yourself, "Is that answer reasonable?" And this brings up another key requisite for improving responsibility-handling abilities:

Know, understand, and apply the principles of sound business management. Practice the art of thinking and reasoning logically and quickly under any business conditions. Develop your ability to rapidly estimate a situation, consider a variety of alternatives quickly, and then arrive at a decision. It is not necessary to wait for real problems to present themselves to get this practice—you can use hypothetical problems by asking yourself such questions as "What would I do if this happened?" "Supposing that right now, X were to take place. What would be my best course of action?" Such mental drills can sharpen your thinking abilities and prepare you for the times when the problems are real and the responsibility to solve them yours. Furthermore, there is an auxiliary benefit in such practice as pointed out by Dr. Albert Edward Wiggam: "By practicing mental arithmetic 20 minutes a day for 20 days, adults can more than double their ability to calculate. By the same token, creative exercise can regain for us much of the imaginative power we have lost through neglect."

Another point to keep in mind in the managing of responsibilities is the need for accuracy and dependability in your communications. Particularly if communications include facts and figures that superiors will use to make their own decisions. Always double check such information, and, if possible, verify the sources by going back to the original form of the information.

In line with the caution to verify facts and figures is the suggestion that you try to anticipate the need for them. If you know of any problem or project that your superior is apt to want action on, or that he is likely to be handed by his superiors, if possible go ahead on your own to gather the needed facts and figures and prepare them for his use. Exercising initiative, in the absence of specific orders, is one way in which you can broaden your experience and gain more confidence in handling responsibilities.

There is, of course, the very real possibility that when you develop a course of action on your own initiative you will select the wrong one. But even this does not necessarily have to be disastrous. As Harold Boeschenstein, president of Owens-Corning Fiberglass Corporation, says, "The wrong course, vigorously pursued, is better than the right one followed in a vacillating manner." The theory is the same as that of the military maxim, "When in doubt, attack." Some positive action, even the wrong one, will at least get you information that may remove the doubt, or indicate what the right action should be. In fact, you can usually learn more from a failure than you can from a success, and if your thinking is generally straight, you will probably not get yourself into any messes that you cannot also get yourself out of.

The final suggestion to a supervisor who seeks to strengthen his relationship to his job is possibly the most important of all: watch your attitude.

Just being willing to accept and face up to problems and difficulties is not enough. You must also learn to manage them or risk that they will take over managing you. Alfred Cooper, writing in the *American Machinist,* pointed out that "the supervisor must always work under stress; every irritating factor in his job adds a bit more to this strain. But every consideration of physical and mental well-being, and the chances of living out a long and useful life, make it imperative for him to find enjoyment in his job."

A supervisor, intent on carrying out his responsibilities, cannot sidestep stress. He must learn to live with it. You cannot enjoy your work until you learn to work smoothly under all kinds of tension. It is sensible, of course, to plan what you will try to do if things break badly. But this can be done as a game—to practice using your innate resourcefulness—rather than in a spirit of worry or dread. Having worked out a possible plan for meeting a difficulty, no useful purpose is then served by any further thinking about it. Certainly not by any further worrying.

Know subordinates: Any executive, by the nature of his job, is dependent upon other people for carrying out the responsibilities he is charged with. The manager must have an intimate knowledge of that part of the organization under his own direct supervision. He must have a thorough knowledge of the capabilities and limitations of each of the people he is dependent upon. Subordinates must be assigned to jobs commensurate with their individual capabilities. Failure to follow this policy results in inefficient operations.

You also owe it to both your subordinates and yourself to encourage them in exercising initiative. And, as you encourage them to use their own imaginations, be generous in giving help and advice if it is requested. At the same time, be sure you also give credit for suggestions and ideas originating in your subordinate group. When you pass along a good idea suggested by someone under you—and give him or her credit for it—you establish yourself as a person big enough to share your success and progress with others. Furthermore, you increase the respect your assistants will have for you as a boss, thereby earning their enthusiastic cooperation in making you still more successful on your job. You also multiply your own value and importance to the company by the number of your people who contribute ideas, instead of being limited by your own imagination and experience.

Every executive should, of course, have a chief assistant capable of substituting or "backstopping" for him at times. This second man must not only be intelligent, loyal, and hard-working, but he must be the type of individual who can work best with his boss—in this case, you. Having selected such a man, or having determined through observation whom he should be, be sure that you then give him both the opportunity and the freedom to grow into the job of assistant in the full sense of the word.

The importance of giving subordinates this freedom to grow was emphatically stated by Don G. Mitchell, former chairman of Sylvania. "Without question," says Mitchell, "one of the best measures of a manager's ability is his ability to *develop* managers—and that means *developing* the manager, not doing his job for him. A good plant manager is an effective measure of his boss. . . . The manager who spends most of his time complaining about the shortcomings of his submanagers isn't much of a manager himself."

The first step in developing an assistant is to make sure that he is always familiar with your current policies and plans. Then just as you have a right to expect superiors to grant you any needed authority to carry out a delegated task, so you must form the habit of granting such authority to your assistant. Only in this way will he be able to acquire the experience and confidence that will make him capable of performing the job. Proper delegation of authority, accompanied by proper supervision, engenders trust, faith, and confidence. It develops initiative and wholehearted cooperation. Reluctance to delegate authority, on the other hand, is often a mark of retarded development in leadership.

Therefore, in telling your assistant, or any other subordinate, what you want done, tell him what to do, but not how to do it. Hold him responsible, in his turn, for the results you expect of him. Delegate and supervise, but do not intervene except when absolutely necessary. Avoid usurping any prerogatives that go with the authority you grant to anyone else to carry out a responsibility.

Problems of the business: The eminent business leader, Bruce Barton, once advised, "Be thankful for your troubles; they're responsible for 90% of your income." Though the exact percentage may be questionable, there is no question that problems make jobs. Usually the more problems connected with a job or a position, the better it pays. And there are many men in business today who are not holding down bigger jobs simply because, without realizing it, they are continually trying to side-step the problems of their present jobs instead of looking upon those troubles for what they are: stepping stones to promotion and better pay.

The hard fact is that there are no trouble-free jobs, any more than there are trouble-free families or trouble-free lives. The executive's need is to learn to live with his problems. It is good to remember, too, that any new or important experience frequently comes disguised as trouble. Acquiring experience may be a painful proposition, but that is what pays big salaries and leads to better positions for executives.

In attacking problems, it is better to adopt some uniform approach to them. Then a new or different problem doesn't present such a frightening prospect—at least you know how to get started on it. This is the basis for the military's "estimate of the situation"—a step-by-step procedure every officer is taught to apply even in the stress of combat situations. In simplified form, the steps are:

1. Determination of the mission—exactly what are you to accomplish?

2. Obtain descriptions of the situation and the alternative courses of action.

3. Analyze opposing courses of action open to the enemy.

4. Compare to your own courses of action.

5. Decide on the action to be taken.

This particular procedure doesn't, of course, lend itself to a literal translation to business problems of every type. Among other weaknesses, it is designed to consider situations where there are only two opponents. In business, of course, "opponents" may be many and varied—even if they are just different interests within the same company. But a similar standard approach to problems is a worthwhile tool for any executive to work out for his own needs to save himself indecision and "wheel-spinning" when asked to take on a new and large amount of responsibility. With practice, the problem-solving executive can hope to reach the proficiency of such men as Ralph Cordiner, whose job of reorganizing and rebuilding the General Electric Company has been described as "the equivalent of trying to rebuild the 20th Century Limited while it was doing 90 miles an hour using the old parts."

A decision, of any kind, involves a choice of alternatives which will, hopefully at least, move you closer to an objective. The objective itself may be a complex one involving a combination of factors which may, in turn, be in actual conflict with one another. And usually, in business, decisions are never certainties. But you can flip a coin and stand a 50-50 chance of being right. Add even a modicum of judgment and imagination to this, and you should be able to raise the odds to 75-25 or even better. And certainly any executive who can be right 75 per cent of the time has nothing to fear from his own decision-making abilities.

Fear, of course, is one of the worst forms of trouble for an executive. All of us fear the unknown to a certain extent. The opposite of fear is courage, which, as Sir Winston Churchill says, "... is the greatest of all assets because it allows all the others to exist."

In working with problems, you will always find some unknowns—some incalculables that involve risk. In these circumstances, the thing to do is adhere to what you think is right and to have the courage of your convictions to at least initiate action. As mentioned, any purposeful action is better than none, or better than vacillating indecision because action at least gets you information.

It will seldom be necessary, under ordinary circumstances,

for you to assume the responsibility for mistakes that are not yours. But if you want to earn the respect of your superiors, win friends in the organization and loyalty among subordinates, make it a rule to promptly "grab the buck" in any situation where the blame is even remotely yours. By so doing, you will not only develop a frank and fearless spirit yourself, you will also build a reputation as a man whose shoulders are broad enough and whose courage is strong enough to assume responsibility even when things go wrong. Fortunately, for the man who is willing to stick his neck out, the observation by Marcus Aurelius still holds true: "Nothing happens to any man which he is not formed by nature to bear."

The future: There are times when the business executive is asked to take on some responsibility that is far beyond any of his previous experience. In such a situation, it is worth remembering that every new problem had to be worked out by someone who was not quite up to it initially. Every big job has to be learned the hard way. In this respect many business problems and decisions are future-oriented—their ultimate most satisfactory conclusion can only be achieved in the future and there will always be an element of the unknown so far as predictable results are concerned.

The future, however, is not stumbled upon. It is created by thoughts and acts. Proper planning ahead will lay the groundwork for sound and timely decisions and will prepare you to accept larger and more important responsibilities as they happen in the yet unknown future. Your ability to reach sound conclusions when dealing with this unknown future will be largely dependent upon the degree of practice you put into making decisions based in the present.

You will also, of course, need a fund of basic knowledge to guide you in making future-oriented decisions. It is probably true that "experience is like the stern lights on a boat; it illuminates only the past." But a fund of experience and acquired knowledge is invaluable in exercising the responsibility of calculating the future risk in a decision.

The late Dr. John Arnold, of Stanford University, often gave businessmen this advice: "Learn facts in a wide variety of fields; develop new areas of interest. Don't study just your books on business administration, or personnel management, or whatever your field may be, but look into new areas. Study cultural anthropology, or the modern dance—I don't care what it is, but learn something new. More important—when you learn something different, somehow try to relate it back to your main area of interest. Ask yourself, 'What can I abstract from this new bit of knowledge, this new area of experience, that somehow may apply to my specialty, my own job?' "

Read the daily newspapers and weekly news magazines; try to evaluate current news impartially and correctly. Check your own evaluations with events as they occur to sharpen your own degree of accuracy. And interpret everything in the light of the effect it will have on your job or industry.

Be alert to trends; listen to enlightened opinions; observe successful decision-makers and those able to take and carry out responsibilities. And if there is something you do not understand, research it out and think about it until you do.

The responsibilities you take today are the experience you will count on tomorrow; the knowledge you acquire today is the background against which you will grow tomorrow.

The executive who wants to prepare himself for major responsibilities could well take as his motto the observation of Abraham Lincoln: "I will prepare myself, and my chance will come."

Today's manager will have a tremendous respect for facts, and a driving desire to obtain the information to reduce the so-called intangibles of business to specific factors that he can weigh and apply intelligently to his problems and his decisions.

4

For Better Managing, Start With Better Information

Managers who have had the experience of starting up a new computer, even one of modest capacity, have frequently been appalled at the voracious appetites such equipment has for information. And if these same executives are also the ones made responsible for digging up the information to satisfy the computer, they may get another shock when they face the realization of just how much of their business has seemingly been conducted on the basis of intuition, hunch, guesswork, and luck.

Consequently, there is a major movement across industry today. It has aptly been described as "the information revolution"—the drive to learn more, to get more facts, and to do more analysis of available information before making any kind of major decision.

While this movement had its beginning in the pioneering computer-oriented business, the effects are now felt all through business—from manufacturers to service organizations and suppliers, and on out to neighborhood retailers (who suddenly find that many of their manufacturers and wholesalers begin to speak different languages on such subjects as volume discounts, promotional allowances, and credit terms.) This, in turn, is forcing retailers and other peripheral companies to become more knowledgeable about their own businesses.

Being knowledgeable, however, requires not only the skill to apply information, but also skill in the ability to collect it efficiently and intelligently in the first place. This chapter deals with four key areas of information handling:

The nature of information as such.

Sources of business information.

Methods of acquiring new information.

Relating information to your problem.

The Nature of Information

Harold Geneen, president of International Telephone & Telegraph Corporation, once said, "Being smart is merely a matter of getting all the facts; once you know everything about a problem, the right answer is obvious."

The problem, for the average person, is to know when he is getting facts, and when he is getting information that only sounds factual. All facts of importance to a management problem usually fall into one of three general classes: statistical, historical, and empirical.

Statistical information consists of enough facts of the same kind to be able to group and count them. As samples, Harold C. Levinson, author of *Chance, Luck, and Statistics,* suggests these:

Statistical information	*Possible use*
Height of American males	In tailoring or coffin manufacturing
Railroad or airline passenger traffic loads	To determine in advance the most probable service requirements

Statistical information	*Possible use*
Sales of items in a retail store or mail-order house	To estimate future demands seasonal selling characteristics, etc.
Birth and death records of a group of the population	To plan specialized life insurance coverages for that group

You will note that these types of statistics are generally available from government census figures, army induction statistics, interstate commerce figures, etc. If you could ever have important uses for this type of information, you may want to consider some form of full-time collecting system to gather such statistics on a continuing basis. Depending on your particular informational needs, the system can be as simple as a manila envelope into which you, or your secretary, puts an occasional newspaper or trade magazine clipping, industry bulletin, company report, etc., on up to a daily updating of a computer data bank.

The choice of which statistics to use on a given problem will have to be made on the basis of the problem. A dress manufacturer, for example, who has always considered his market as the female population of the United States, will find that, even statistically, there is a tremendous variety of females. Furthermore, their desirability as marketing targets grows or diminishes depending on the classification he puts them in: economic groupings; ages; dress sizes; geographical locations; marital status; or any combinations of these. In other words, before he can apply statistical information, he must first make a judgment as to which set of facts he will select to work with. In order to do this he may have to add some historical information on his past sales to even begin to figure out which types of dresses he can profitably produce to effectively sell to any given grouping of women.

This same basic problem also affects the retailer of the dresses. Before he can decide what styles and sizes he should order from the manufacturer, he must first analyze his customers and prospects on the basis of what they will buy. All retailers do this, of course—but usually on an "instinct" basis, which is why the retailer clearance sale is so popular for disposing of unpurchased items. To do it intelligently requires information, most of which is already in the retailer's files or books covering the history of his business.

Often decisions must be made on problems where there is no previous track record—either statistical or historical. This is particularly true in production and development type situations where the problems just happen—and someone has to come up with the information that will lead to a solution. Usually the best available information, then, is *empirical:* just what you can see by taking a good look.

On-the-spot inspections are a favorite technique of nationally known problem-solver James Rand, president of Cleveland's Rand Development Corporation. Rand once solved a problem that had been bugging experts on iron ore shipping for several years. He did it by making a personal inspection of Mesabi Range railheads in the freezing cold of winter. By actually seeing what was going on, rather than trying to solve the problem in theory from the warm comfort of a design office, he was able to suggest a change in the equipment on a conveyor belt so that ore particles froze before they went into the hopper cars rather than after. This prevented the ore from becoming frozen to the cars so that it would not dump out into ship loading bins at the end of the trip from the mines. Rand's cold day's journey was worth money both to the ore shippers and to Rand himself.

The secret of collecting empirical knowledge quickly and efficiently is probably that of thinking through to some viewpoint before you begin to ask questions. This was the advice given to Thomas Jones, president of Northrop Corporation, by his father. "Always try," said his father, "to understand what is behind this; what is at the bottom of that. Always look for the key, and then build detail around it."

Sources of Information

In this day of instant communication, it is never a problem to find some information on almost any subject you can think of. Sources of information abound. The consideration in collecting information should be on the degree of efficiency possible—how to learn the most in the least amount of time. For example, if you want just a simple definition of a word, the first place to look should be your desk dictionary. If this doesn't tell you enough, then go to some more comprehensive source, an unabridged dictionary or encyclopedia. If you need still more information, consult a specialized reference on the particular subject. It is the same with other information: you start with yourself, then spread out if your own resources are not sufficient. Here are common sources of information in the order of their ease of availability:

Your own knowledge, based on your own experience. Your own experience and knowledge of a subject, if properly acquired, are as valuable as anyone else's when you first start to gather information. And by relying on yourself from the first, you will be in a much better position to make the final judgments that lead to better decisions.

As Rudyard Kipling once said in an interview with Arthur Gordon, "The individual has always had to struggle to keep from being overwhelmed by the tribe. To be your own man is a hard business. If you try it, you'll be lonely often, and sometimes frightened. But no price is too high to pay for the privilege of owning yourself."

Relying on first-hand knowledge has been one of the keys to success of entrepreneur-inventor Sherman Fairchild. The story is related of how a few years ago he became interested in the stock of a midwestern growth company. Fairchild called his broker to tell him to start buying. "They asked me if I didn't want to see the balance sheets of the company," he relates. "I said no; I've met their people and that is good enough for me. Everyone I met seemed to know his business, what the company objectives were, and how they proposed to get there. Why look at books? In a growth company you need people with vision and organization."

Other peoples' knowledge, based on their experience. Judgment must begin to enter into an information gathering effort the minute you turn outside your own knowledge and experience and begin to depend on others. There are times when you must take another person's word as good judgment and accept it. Representative Vinson, former chairman of the House Armed Services Committee, once explained why he didn't always "give the Committee unlimited time for the consideration of every problem." He said, "Why, if you wanted to, you could spend hours discussing the extension of an aircraft runway. You have to have some faith in the people who propose these things. They are trying to achieve the same results for America which we are trying to achieve. If a runway has to be a hundred feet longer, it has to be."

Public records form another source of generally available information. It has been estimated that 10 per cent to 30 per cent of a scientific project's cost can be saved by gathering and interpreting the literature already available. Much information that any executive will need is already available in his company's existing records—though he may need the equivalent of a fact-finding bloodhound to track it down.

The reason it is difficult to locate such information is that usually the facts were first collected for some entirely different purpose, and will be filed or stored under some classification related to that purpose rather than to your immediate needs. You must therefore be able to identify and ask for information functionally, without knowing what its original source may have been. For example, if you are thinking of a new guarantee offer on a product or service, you will want facts on the actual reliability of your products in the past. Unless someone has been collecting reliability figures per se, you will probably have to resort to other types of information entirely. One possibility would be to examine customer complaint files and the field reports of how the complaints were satisfied. This information, with some imaginative interpretation, could be a completely satisfactory substitute for actual reliability figures.

It is easy, when on a quest for information, to forget such sources as your public library, the United States government, and trade and industry associations. Some of this is probably due to the common feeling every person with a problem has that his problem is unique, and no one else ever had it before. But the fact is that other people with interests similar to yours will have similar problems. Some of them may have solved a particular problem and let the result be known. In which case, it is undoubtedly recorded in some accessible document.

One particularly valuable source of continuing information on business problems of all types is the U. S. Government Printing Office. Every business concern should have at least one person on the mailing list to receive the periodic bulletins of new offerings by this organization. This person can then pass on news of new offerings to others who may have need of the particular types of information. It is true that you frequently have to wade through dozens of listings of such esoteric subjects as "Geology of the Reliz Canyon, Thompson Canyon, and San Lucas Quadrangles, Monterey County, California," in order to find a few such gems as "Maintaining Work Flow" and "Fundamentals of PERT," but the descriptive bulletins are free, the publications are modestly priced, and you pay only for the information you actually order.[1]

The "last resort" type of information should certainly be that obtained from original research. This is not to decry original research in those fields such as science, economics, sociology, and such. But most business problems can be solved without this most expensive of information gathering techniques. If, however, all other resources fail, and you still cannot locate the information you need from existing sources, then do what is necessary: go after your own original information.

There are times when imagination can help you cut the costs or gain time in finding original information. When Henry Kaiser decided to set up his privately endowed Foundation Health Plan, he needed some cost figures on the average man's insurance rates for prepaid doctoring. He turned the job of determining these over to his regular staff of engineers, feeling that their analytical and mathematical talents were as good as anyone else's, and he already had them on the payroll.

Methods of Acquiring New Information

The first step in going after new information is to prepare a summary of what you already know, and a comparable summary of what you need to know. This is the key to

[1] To be put on the mailing list for bulletins, write: U.S. Government Printing Office, Division of Public Documents, Washington, D.C., 20402

isolating the specific questions to be answered, and determining just who it is that can be considered as sources of answers. Such a step is also necessary because it may, of itself, suggest alternatives among courses of action. In describing past Pentagon problems in R.&D., Secretary of Defense Robert McNamara said, "We have often paid too little attention to how a proposed weapon system would be used and what it would cost and, finally, whether the contribution the development could make to our forces would be worth the cost." As a result, new approaches were initiated in R.&D. projects, all of which revolve around better planning to collect necessary information "before we start 'bending metal'."

According to Harvey M. Wagner, an authority on statistical controls, this problem is also faced by managers who turn to operations research techniques in search of new answers to problems. "OR typically substitutes one set of management problems for another, often more complex, set," says Wagner. "Consequently, an executive tottering at the brink of undertaking an OR approach is well advised to consider which set of problems he would rather face.... Specifically, in many instances, the company must develop new systems and procedures of implementing the OR approach, raise the level of technical skills of personnel, and maintain a staff competent to operate and modify the system as future needs dictate. All of these factors," he points out, "usually lead to increased overhead burden."

A critical question in launching a project of original research is in knowing who to ask. For example, an airline seeking ways to improve its service might hire the services of a national research organization to go into the field and query customers, potential customers, and nonflyers. North Central Airlines, however, decided that the people most in touch with the day-to-day needs of the airline customers were the flight crews. This resulted in what the line calls their "Discrepancy Book," in which pilots and stewardesses are asked to note briefly any unusual occurrences in flight at the first station they reach, as well as anything else they feel should be brought to the attention of executives and supervisors. This includes good ideas and practices as well as complaints. In commenting on the value of this form of continuing research, North Central President Hal N. Carr says, "The flying people are the eyes and ears of an airline. They are in touch with our customers daily, and can observe the operation at many different places. If they see a good idea in practice at one point, they usually bring about its adoption at other places."

Once the decisions are made as to what information is still needed, and who the best source of information will probably be, the next step is to develop an information collecting plan. A key step in this is to put down the objective of the project. Prepare a statement in writing of just why you feel the research is being initiated, and what you expect to get out of it. Then get the agreement, preferably also in writing, of everyone else who will have to accept or use the information once it is generated.

The reason for this is purely in the interest of insuring understanding. A search for new information will usually be probing into unknown areas where even language can trip you up. Dr. MacDonald Critchley, senior physician of Queen's Square National Hospital, London, explained this problem as it applies in science: "Nowadays," he said, "the growth of ideas and knowledge has so outstripped the growth of our vocabulary that there is always a very real danger of developing confusion, so that the language employed by scientists runs a very real risk of being not fully comprehended not only by the world at large, but by other scientists in the same discipline, and, of course, in other disciplines also."

Another key step in collecting new information is to break your big questions down into small ones. In the General Electric Company's value engineering courses, students are given a course project of cutting the costs of an electric motor by 30 per cent. They are first taught, however, to stop thinking of the motor as a finished unit, and to begin thinking of it as a series of smaller components which can be questioned for their individual values in the whole. The data furnished to the students gives a further summary of how the problem is broken down:

Present costs of each component in the motor.

Names of present vendors.

Drawings and specifications.

Estimated quantities of components used each year.

Materials specified.

Design and performance data.

Planning and manufacturing paperwork and control procedures.

Present methods of fabrication and assembly.

Manufacturing cost and time data.

Working from this detailed breakdown of cost items, the General Electric engineers then go to work to systematically question each individual item. This type of breakdown can be applied to almost any management problem as well. It should never be: "Find out about costs." Rather, "What are our fixed manufacturing costs?... our variable manufacturing costs?... our labor costs?... overhead?... sales costs? etc." Then each of these questions is further subdivided and asked and answered one at a time.

If your information quest involves other people, as it usually will, some thought should be given as to how you can make the desired information easy to give. This may involve trying different forms of a question to make sure you have one that cannot be misunderstood. Sample questions can be submitted to others in your organization to determine how people not familiar with your problem will respond to the various versions you are testing.

Questioning is a problem in communications. Dr. William S. Howell, professor of speech, University of Minnesota, says, "An executive too often tends to ignore the strong possibility that what he told a subordinate is unclear. He does not listen or watch for the other's response. He has fallen into the 'pitfall of projection' where he assumes that others know what he is thinking, or that they have his knowledge about a particular problem."

Once you have tested your questions on an informal basis, and selected those that seem to yield the kind of information you need, the questions themselves should then be organized into a logical-sequence prepared questionnaire. Even if your technique will be to interview people personally, prepare the questionnaire. Having the questions down in writing is a way to make certain that you don't forget to ask the important ones, and don't become distracted by something in the interview itself so that you forget the tested forms of your questions.

As you begin the job of collecting answers, you can concurrently begin to weigh and evaluate the information that is coming in. This means constantly testing the information to determine if it is responsive to your needs. Dr. Ralph Nichols, coauthor of the book *Are You Listening?*, has these suggestions which apply equally well to evaluating responses to questions: "Weigh the speaker's evidence by mentally questioning it. As he presents facts, illustrative stories, and statistics, ask yourself: 'Are they accurate? Do they come from an unprejudiced source? Am I getting the full picture, or is he telling me only what will prove his point?' "

Another technique that is often helpful is that of collecting and refining by revision. You start with an original plan, begin to ask your questions, and then, as the information comes in, try to form some tentative conclusions which can be checked in the latter stages of the project. The original plan can be modified in favor of verifying or elaborating particularly interesting key information produced early in the study. As Howard S. Nutting, head of Dow Chemical Company's research index, points out, "Analytical ability is 75% of the job and intuition is the other 25%."

How to Relate Information to the Problem

The real test of the value of any information you generate lies in its application and relationship to the problem. Therefore, the job of relating the information should actually begin before the facts start coming in.

If you properly prepare the problem in the first place, you will have some framework or mental outline of the informational holes in your understanding. Then, as the facts begin coming in, you try to match information to need to determine where each new piece of information lines up with a part of the problem. A simple technique for organizing information consists of putting each separate fact or important bit of information on an individual 3 x 5 or 4 x 6 card. When all the cards are prepared, you can organize, arrange, and rearrange the facts into related or comparable pairs, sequences, or groupings by simply shuffling them around. Once your desired sequences have been developed, the cards are then transcribed by your secretary into any arrangement that will make analysis easy for you.

Finally, in every information gathering activity, the time comes when you must put your findings to work—you must attempt to use the information in some way, usually to arrive at a decision on a course of action. If the problem is one where the risk is slight and the foreseeable consequences can be controlled, then the easiest way to verify your facts may simply be to make the decision and take the indicated action.

On the other hand, if the consequences of having wrong

information or incomplete information could be serious, a better plan is to attempt a "paper" solution to the problem: write up a proposal just as you think the situation can or should be handled and then submit it to a group for a critique to see if it makes as much sense to them as it does to you. The United States military makes good use of this technique by means of what they frankly call "murder boards." Any major new proposal dealing with unknown or little known factors is submitted to a board, which attempts to tear the proposal to pieces and find every flaw. If they find enough, the proposal goes back to its sponsor for more thinking.

To summarize: Gathering a full fact-file of meaningful information on which to base a decision is not always easy. Usually the more important the decision, the more difficult to get sufficient information to be sure you have covered all the bases. But information gathering can be efficient if it is planned and if a continuing effort is made to evaluate it and relate it to the problem at hand right from the start.

To paraphrase Peter Drucker's classic statement on executive efficiency, "There is nothing so useless as doing efficiently that which should not be done at all," we can rightfully say that "There is no activity more wasteful than diligently learning that which has no value to anyone."

The manager must understand innovation. Even though he may not be a highly creative person himself, he must be able to encourage and direct creativity on the part of others, for it is only through innovation that a company can continue to grow and progress.

5

Encourage Innovation

Usually when we think about an innovation in business, it is in terms of some idea. Therefore, any study of innovating should probably start with what makes a good idea. The simplified dictionary definition of an idea is "a concept; also, a precept. A design; a preliminary plan; often a plan or purpose of action; project."

Broad as this definition is, it offers scant encouragement to the manager who may be considering a risk of dollars and time to try out some new idea that he or one of his employees may have. The man attempting to evaluate a possible idea for his business needs something more tangible and practical in the way of criteria to measure the possibilities in a new proposal.

There are three areas in which business ideas are usually found:

Management ideas, which include ways to utilize better the four tools of the manager: people, money, time, and facilities.

Product ideas, involving ways to increase the function, utility, performance, or salability of the products or services sold.

People ideas are those which involve improving the selection, orientation, training, or supervision of the people at all levels of the organization.

Considering the current high interest that businessmen are showing in government and politics domestically, and the expanding interest in international affairs and trade, a fourth area for ideas is certainly suggested: those pertaining to the businessman's *environment:* his community, city, state, nation, and even the world.

Anyone who has ever experienced the job of making a decision on a new proposal in any of these areas will realize immediately that all new ideas are not good simply because they are new. How then to recognize the good from the bad, to sort out the possibles from the probables? In other words, just how can you tell if you really have an idea for a worthwhile innovation?

A more practical definition of an idea, at least from the manager's standpoint, is this: an idea represents a possible solution to some problem, or the possible satisfaction of an opportunity. By extension, then, a "good" idea is one that instead of just presenting a possibility, will definitely fill a need (which may or may not have been expressed up to the time the idea was presented).

Specifically, a good idea which will fill a business need will generally satisfy one or more of the following criteria: it will increase production; improve quality; present a more efficient utilization of manpower; improve methods in general; offer a way to improve present tools or machinery; reduce costs; improve office methods or working conditions.

Note that the term "improvement" appears often in these standards. If a proposal does not offer an improvement in an existing situation, chances are it is not really worthwhile as an idea—at least in the sense that businessmen are interested in ideas. Here are specific illustrations of ideas in each of the criteria categories that have either solved problems or offered improvements in a variety of situations:

Ideas that increase productivity are usually improvements in methods or equipment that let an individual accomplish more in less time or with less effort. Examples of such ideas, currently coming into widespread usage, include such simple mechanization ideas as a "powered" wheelbarrow for moving heavy loads of concrete on major construction jobs; using pressure-sensitive tape, which sticks by itself, instead of string, which must be tied, to assemble an electrical or electronic wiring harness; use of electronic devices to guard large areas such as stores, warehouses, plant yards, etc. These permit one guard, at a central station, to monitor the security of vast establishments on a continuous basis.

The ultimate in increasing production for many industries has, of course, been the introduction of automation. In fact, there is no longer anything new in the idea of automating a plant or production facility. There are, however, new approaches to the human factors in implementing automation being developed constantly. The National Biscuit Company, for example, demonstrated such an approach in the application of automation in a new Chicago bakery. They invited employees and union representatives of two existing plants to suggest improvements on a model of the proposed new plant that would replace the two inefficient facilities. By so doing, the company earned the support and help of the affected workers to the point where the transition was carried out smoothly enough that following the start of the new plant, business increased to the point that one-third more workers were subsequently hired.

Ideas that improve quality will usually be thought of in terms of products, but they can also involve the work standards of clerical and white collar employees as well. In terms of products, such ideas will usually contribute either to a longer life, a better performance, or a more economical operation for the product. In terms of people, they are usually motivational or educational steps that raise performance levels, eliminate errors, and instill a pride in craftsmanship. Many product-quality ideas result from sheer necessity. For example, it was the need for more reliable electronic components for missiles and other airborne equipment that led to the development of printed circuits and the now generally accepted solid state circuits.

In some cases, quality improvements come out of possibilities released by newly developed materials or technologies. An example is the gradual replacement of linoleum and other quick-wearing floor coverings by vinyl and plastics in general.

Many quality improvements stem from competitive pressures. The first water-soluble wall paints, for instance, filled a need for an easy-to-apply, quick-drying change of color. But as they won general acceptance, competition among paint manufacturers led to development after development —each step being a new idea or concept—until the present array of rubber base and the newly arriving plastic bases became available. Each such development further increased the quality of the color coating and, in some cases, resulted in functional improvements as well.

Ideas aimed at achieving a more efficient utilization of manpower are closely related to ideas that increase productivity, but usually revolve around the performance of an individual, rather than a machine or other piece of equipment. Some may come out of an analysis of the jobs which people are expected to perform. For example, many companies still follow the policy of expecting their sales force to call on any and every possible prospect in their territories. Other companies have analyzed their customer and prospect list and found that the bulk of their business, as high as 85 per cent in some instances, comes from as few as 10-25 per cent of their accounts. By applying the simple principle of investment and return, a much more effective utilization of a salesman's time can be made.

Other ideas for making better use of people stem from an analysis of the overall manpower needs of the organization. Minnesota Mining and Manufacturing Company, for instance, analyzed their management payroll over a five-year period and found there was a definite correlation between sales and the number of managers in each of several critical classifications. They have since followed the practice of applying their sales forecasts to personnel forecasts to predict the number of executives and scientists who will be needed for future growth and management continuity. Experience has proved the formula to be accurate within 1 per cent of actual needs. This practice lets them follow specific hiring policies and build individualized development programs for younger executives to make sure they will have the management talents they need when the company needs them. Still other ideas aimed at satisfying the need to utilize manpower at most effective levels include the use of company planes to expedite executive travel; company financing of advanced educational programs related to a man's work needs; shirt-pocket "Pagette" type radio receivers for instant locating of salesmen, route men, and service repairmen; and even the instant convenience-type foods, which let the executive's wife utilize her free time in more productive ways than spending it all in the kitchen.

Ideas that improve methods can be found in several areas. They may involve operations; the way, for instance, many independent food stores now compete with the big chains by utilizing the techniques of centralized buying and cooperative advertising. They may involve improvements in maintenance procedures, an example being the new method of constructing major electronic systems with individual components or subcomponents built on modular principles. A troublesome part can be removed completely, and replaced *in toto,* to be repaired later. So much attention is being paid to maintainance procedures these days, largely because of the high cost of downtime for key equipment, that many original equipment manufacturers are beginning to make a maintenance engineer a part of their design team in the development of new products.

Another area for improved methods is that of construction. New materials and new building techniques have already made most standard construction methods of even ten years ago nearly obsolete. New construction ideas include such concepts as the windowless factory, which with present-day air conditioning and illumination methods, may actually be both cheaper and more satisfactory than a windowed structure. Still other construction savings are found in the realm of sheer ingenuity. A prime example was the construction of the Albuquerque, New Mexico, civic auditorium. The structure was planned to utilize a reinforced concrete dome for the roof. The way it was achieved was to build up a hill existing on the site to the desired height and conformation for the inside of the dome. The hilltop was then used as a base, over which the concrete was poured. The supporting columns were constructed in a trench dug under the rim of the dome, and the hill was then moved out, leaving the domed structure supported on its columns. A precedent testing case of constructing a building from the roof down!

Shop type ideas are those which may result in improvements in present tooling or machinery. In many cases, these ideas also result from necessity. With investments in production tools and machines being as heavy as they are today, few companies can afford to scrap their capital investments every time engineering comes up with a new material or a new machining need. Usually the production department will find themselves continually being called upon to produce ideas that will increase the function of present tools and machines, or give them more flexibility or utility to meet new needs. As one means of satisfying such increasing demands, new types of low-cost tracer controls and sensors are now available which can be applied to existing milling machines, borers, and large lathes to give them sensitivities and capabilities to work to more demanding specifications. Tooling, too, is in a constant state of improvement due to demands of new materials. To a certain extent, the widespread usage of titanium is still being blocked by the difficulties of working it on mass-production basis, and efforts so far to develop low-cost, safe methods of cutting, shaping, and grinding it have not yielded the ideas that are needed.

Ideas that increase safety fall into two general classes. Usually safety is thought of in terms of the human equation—eliminating hazards to the lives and limbs of people. But under the "safety" heading should also go those ideas aimed at protecting work in progress from accidental damage. This same grouping would also include those ideas aimed at reducing worker abuse or misuse of costly machines and tools. A simple example of this is the governor used to control the speed at which a company truck or car can be operated. Other ideas in this category range out to such an esoteric one as the installation of a plastic shield between the operator of a high-precision milling machine and his work piece for close tolerance machining. The shield is not to protect the worker, but to deflect his body heat and prevent it from upsetting the accuracy of the cutting equipment he is working with!

Safety for personnel has, of course, made great strides in every field. There are few companies, whether manufacturing, retail, or service, who do not pay some attention to problems of worker safety—if only to enjoy the benefits of lower insurance rates. However, American workers still do lose fingers, arms, legs, and even lives in preventable industrial accidents, and this area of business still offers good hunting to the person looking for opportunities to contribute new ideas.

Ideas that eliminate unnecessary work will frequently be welcomed by the affected workers as well as management. For example, the same National Biscuit Company automated bakery mentioned previously included a mechanized lift to raise 75-lb pieces of dough from table-level to an overhead hopper. A union official was quoted as being in favor of that piece of equipment because "a short guy was apt to rupture himself on that job!"

Other types of work-eliminating ideas may be in the methods area, such as the practice of counting quantities of small parts and hardware items by weight, rather than individually; testing random samplings of items from long production runs, rather than each individual piece as it comes off the line; and planning of salesmen's and routemen's schedules to eliminate backtracking and lost waiting time on stops. Waste motion, waste effort, and waste time all cost real dollars in this day of high labor costs. These areas alone offer unlimited opportunities for idea men who can show that their ideas will eliminate unnecessary work.

Ideas that can be shown to definitely reduce costs are always welcome—in manufacturing, distribution, servicing, and maintenance. Cost-saving ideas include such tangibles as the suggestion by the General Electric Company value engineer who suggested substituting an electric clock part costing one-fifth of a cent for one that was costing the company one-third of a cent. In a year's production, this one change is reported to have saved General Electric $112,000. At the other end of the scale is the new quality-manufacturing concept being introduced into some automobile production plants. Auto manufacturers have lately begun to pay attention to the dealer charge-backs they were getting for repairing, adjusting, and otherwise completing the factory job on new car deliveries. The new quality concept is simply to do a better job of building a new car in the factory to cut the total costs of satisfying the customer.

Other cost-cutting ideas to make news recently include the conversion from metal cans to plastic containers by a liquid detergent manufacturer who admitted that plastic was more expensive now, but would soon be cheaper and, therefore, as long as he was installing new filling equipment anyway, he would shoot for the long-term savings. Still another newsmaker is the burgeoning growth of the inflatable structures business. Today warehouses, maintenance shacks, and even retail stores are in quarters consisting of nylon domes, inflated by low-pressure blowers to provide temporary, or portable, enclosures which would not be economical or practical with permanent structures.

A category of ideas eagerly sought after today are those that will *improve office methods.* Many such improvements can come from imaginative office workers. Like the mail clerk in an insurance company who eliminated the annoying problem of trying to track down letters and other paperwork in the process of being routed through the office. Her method was to make a dry copy of any original letter or memo with a routing list on it; route the copy and file the original. From then on, anyone who wanted a quick look at the letter was able to get a second dry copy while the first one continued on its way.

One of the big problems in measuring ideas for office methods is that business still doesn't really know what can be expected of office workers. This was behind the organization of a cooperative effort among more than eighty large companies by the American Management Association. These companies have agreed to swap data on work loads and accomplishments of white collar workers in an attempt to generate some base statistics on just how many workers it should really take, and what to expect of them, to conduct efficient and effective purchasing, accounting, and personnel management functions. This study, in itself, represents a major idea in the area of office management methods.

Ideas that improve working conditions can range in value from such a simple one as a better quality of paper cup for a coffee machine on out to comprehensive plant planning that embodies the latest in time-motion efficiency as well as psychological findings in the human factors of work output. However, most such ideas in the average plant will concern themselves with improvements to be made in relatively commonplace conditions: environmental noise levels, safety, atmospheric contamination, sanitation, etc. Although air conditioning is widely accepted in theaters, restaurants, and retail stores in this country, it is still not generally accepted for manufacturing plants. And further improvements in atmosphere control (as opposed to simple comfort control) are now possible through new developments like electronic air cleaners, which remove dust, pollen, and other contaminants to make for a cleaner, less irritating working environment.

Even the use of colors in manufacturing areas to ease eye strain and operator fatigue by color coding operational parts is a major step in improving working conditions. And, of course, as manufacturing processes get more complex, and as new and different materials are introduced into industry, there will, of necessity, be many new ideas needed to keep the working conditions compatible with the needs, desires, and requirements of the human beings who will be doing the work.

It is apparent that the job of pre-evaluating a new idea to determine its worth is not always an easy one. But then, few aspects of decision-making are easy. In general, however, if the proposal seems to offer a real promise of providing an improvement over an existing condition or situation, it is probably worth trying. The important point is that having ideas, by itself, is never enough. Every promising idea must be given a chance to prove itself if it is to provide an ultimate benefit to anyone. And frequently the quickest way to test the value of a new idea—or to determine if you really have an idea at all—is simply to try it.

The manager will also understand ideas—those nebulous and relative contributions individual efforts make to the success of the whole.

Increase Your Own Idea Production

Fortunately, the ability to produce ideas is not an exclusive talent of just a few lucky people. Everyone has some ability to think up ideas—in fact, we are all *born* with it. If you doubt this, just think for a moment about some child you know who is between the ages of four and six. Chances are, if you encourage him at all, this youngster can spin you the wildest yarns, right out of his imagination. You could do it too when you were his age. Every youngster has this ability to imagine.

However, in the normal process of growing up, imagination tends to get sidetracked. We begin to learn, for instance, that many of the things we have been imagining just aren't so. Then, as we go through school, we are taught to absorb factual knowledge—the kind where an answer can only be right or wrong. We begin to develop what is generally known as "judgment." By the time a man reaches the age and degree of experience to be thinking about managing a company, chances are his judgment is one of his strongest qualities. However, judgment is just the opposite of imagination. The better we become at judging and making decisions, the less apt we are to exercise our imagination. But the ability to imagine is always there. All you have to do is remember that it is, call on it when you have a problem or an opportunity, and give it a chance.

But is there actually a way to release your imagination to increase your production of ideas? More specifically, can you increase your production of *good* ideas? Many scientists, educators, and psychologists are now convinced, on the basis of an impressive weight of evidence, that you can. And thousands of adults who have participated in creative thinking and problem solving courses and institutes sponsored by adult evening schools, colleges, universities, and business and governmental organizations are also satisfied that it can be done.

In this chapter we will explore some of the types of exercises used to demonstrate differences in thinking methods as they are taught in such courses. These exercises have been adapted for your individual use in the privacy of your home or office. You should find them fun and, possibly, quite rewarding.

The only equipment you will need are a pencil, paper, and some type of timing device such as a three-minute egg timer or a kitchen timer that can ring a bell at the end of three minutes. (If you only have a watch or conventional clock, better have someone else time the three-minute periods for you. You will need to concentrate too closely on your paper to keep close track of time also.)

There are two sets of problems. Each set is preceded by simple instructions and followed by an analysis. It is suggested that you complete No. 1, including the analysis, before going on to No. 2.

SET NO. 1: Complete these before
reading further

Instructions: For each of the three following questions, see how many *good* ideas you can list in a three-minute time period. *Do not put down any idea unless you think it is good enough to have real value. This is important*—your total

score for this section will be the total number of *good* ideas
you can list for the three problems.

1. List all the *good* uses you can for an ordinary kitchen
   broom other than sweeping. (three minutes)
2. You are the owner of a downtown building. There is only
   one doorway through which everyone enters and leaves
   at noontime. This causes a congestion problem. What
   good and completely satisfactory ways can you think of
   to alleviate this situation? (three minutes)
3. The United States government now conducts a major
   program of public relations and promotion aimed at
   encouraging more foreign travelers to visit the United
   States as tourists. The long-range success of this program
   will, of course, depend to a large extent on the kinds of
   impressions such visitors take back with them. Your
   problem is this: List all the *good* ideas you can think of
   that the average person could do to help a visitor to this
   country understand and appreciate the United States
   better. (three minutes)

(Total and write down the number of good ideas you have
listed for all three questions.)

Now, let's consider what you have accomplished so far.
Chances are you have some ideas for each of those three
problems. The next question is what do you think of your
own ideas?

Do you feel that any of them are particularly original, or
are they the kinds of suggestions almost anyone would think
of?

In applying the instructions to list only "good" ideas, how
many ideas did you have that you did not list because, in

your opinion, they would not work? Or would be too expensive? Or they were too academic? Or somebody would have thought of it before if it were any good? These are common and usual reasons for rejecting ideas when we are trying to evaluate them quickly—and, of course, you were told to do just that. The purpose of this set of exercises was to demonstrate how such cautionary reasoning acts as a brake or restriction on really making full use of your imagination. And we all have such brakes to some degree.

There are, in general, two types of restrictions that any average person will apply to his imagination: *inner* blocks, which keep him from presenting his ideas because he doesn't have enough confidence in their value; and *external* blocks, which make him hesitate to offend or contradict or otherwise upset someone else—his boss, a fellow worker, a customer, his wife, etc. Both types have the final effect of causing us to inhibit our imagination and slow down our total output of ideas. Furthermore, they prevent us from producing as many good ideas as we could.

This next series of problems is aimed at seeing what could happen if you freed yourself from any mental restrictions whatever in producing ideas. In other words, suspend that judgment you used to determine if an idea is good or not. You may not find this easy to do under the time limits imposed, but it can be done.

SET NO. 2: Do these only *after* you
        have completed the first set
Instructions: In this set, you should again give yourself three

minutes on each problem to list your ideas. But this time *list every idea that comes to you*—wild, mild, good, bad, or indifferent. List these ideas *without judging them in any way*. Forget about quality entirely—your final score will be on the total *quantity* of ideas for the three problems.

1. List all the uses you can think of for a used plastic belt from a dictating machine. (three minutes)
2. You live on a corner lot and people keep walking across the grass, spoiling your lawn. What are all the things you can think of that might solve this problem? (three minutes)
3. The United States government tourist promotion is something that has been discussed for several years. President Eisenhower was in favor of it and, on at least one occasion, he spoke out in favor of "methods by which people can gradually learn a little bit more about each other." Here is your problem: List all the ways you can think of to help yourself learn more about people in foreign lands. (three minutes)

(Write down your total number of ideas on this set of problems.)

Now study the lists of ideas you have just completed. Note the quantity of ideas and compare it to the first set. It should, of course, be much larger for Set No. 2.

But now ask the same questions about the second list that you asked about your ideas on the first list. Are there a few more original ideas among your suggestions for these problems? Are there some potentially good ideas or more interesting ideas on the second set of lists that you might not have put down if you had been trying to list only the really good ones?

Chances are your second set of idea lists—where you were simply listing ideas without trying to evaluate them—will contain not only more ideas in quantity than the first set, but it will also contain more good or quality ideas than when these were all you were trying to list.

This becomes more significant when you consider that the six problems presented were actually matched pairs—the first problem in Set No. 1 was no more difficult than the first problem in Set No. 2. The same is true of questions two and three in both sets. With the difficulty of the questions being the same, and the time you spent on each problem also the same, the only variable, then, was in the method of thinking presented to you in the instructions. In other words, whether or not you were trying to judge the ideas as you listed them.

These problems, and the results obtained from following the two types of instructions, are similar to the problems used and the results obtained in scientific research studies at the University of Buffalo. This research, conducted with the aid of the Creative Education Foundation, has also been validated by similar research at other leading universities.

The Buffalo studies found that students who were participating in the research project consistently produced more good ideas when they suspended their judgment than when they tried to evaluate the ideas as they went along. The method of researching this conclusion was this:

Persons participating in the studies were presented with pairs of problems under the two types of instructions, evaluative and nonevaluative, and produced their idea lists. Raters of the research team then scored the ideas on a six-point scale: three for usefulness and three for uniqueness (how "different" the idea was). An arbitrarily high standard of five points was established for an idea to be termed "good." In the process, the raters canceled out any ideas on an individual's list which essentially duplicated an idea previously listed. After all ideas were scored, final scores were obtained by counting up the total number of five-point or "good" ideas.

Under the instructions to suspend judgment—which you were given for the second set of problems—nearly twice the number of good ideas per individual were produced as under the instructions to evaluate the ideas and list only the good ones, as you were given for the first set of questions.

What happened if you did not produce either more or better ideas on the second set of questions? Chances are you did not quite make it to the "freewheeling" stage where you had really taken the brakes off your imagination. Suspending judgment—even temporarily—takes practice. A lifetime of habits of any kind cannot always be set aside simply by reading an instruction to do so. Also some people have a well-entrenched resistance to the idea that they should ever turn off their judgment at all, even temporarily.

Yet we have two kinds of judgment to steer us through life: that which is conscious and deliberate, and that which is in the subconscious. This subconscious judgment, except in cases of definite mental imbalance, continues to operate for us at all times. The judgment you have to suspend in the creative process is that which has been consciously built up over the years and which you usually bring to bear deliberately. It consists largely of past experience, precedent, and a judgment of the known facts in a situation. But such factors are known to be prime inhibitors of creativity. And, when you want to go after ideas, it is these mental restrictions you should attempt to turn off. And this can be done with the confidence that the unconscious judgment will still be operative.

One example will demonstrate this. An instructor in a creative thinking course uses an exercise which consists of showing the class a plain cardboard box about the size and shape of a cigar box. The box is taped shut; there is no printing or design to reveal the contents. Students are told the box contains a solid, physical object and are asked to suggest items that this could be. They are allowed to hold the box, shake it (the object is taped to the bottom!), smell it—do anything but open it. With no external guides to help, the guesses, of course, range all over the spectrum. Many are humorous (lady's undergarment); some exotic (meteorite dust); some pedestrian (sheet of writing paper). No conscious judgment can be applied because there are no precedents, experience, or supplementary facts supplied.

However, in all such tests involving several hundred students over a period of years, never once has anything been suggested that could not be within the box (such as a liquid or lead shot)—a demonstration that the subconscious governor was always operative in the minds of the students.

Actually, no one in the field of creative education is trying to do away with judgment. It is just that all research to date leads to the conclusion that you can produce more ideas and better ideas if you separate your idea-getting from your evaluation applying.

Dr. Alex F. Osborn, founder and now chairman of the Creative Education Foundation, and author of the book, *Applied Imagination,* sums it up rather neatly when he points out that trying to produce ideas while you judge them is like trying to drive a car with the brakes on.

"But," he also points out, "if we are going to equip a car with a more powerful motor (imagination), we should also equip it with stronger brakes (evaluation)."

"However," he adds, "when we want to produce ideas, the way to go about it is to think up—then judge."

You also have a better chance of solving problems, or producing real innovations, if you adopt some type of systematic approach to the job of going after ideas. Here is the outline for one such approach as presented in many of the courses in problem solving:

1. *Define your problem.* This simply means to know what it is you are trying to accomplish. Be sure you really understand the problem. As an example of why this is important, how many times have you heard someone say something like, "Gosh, the boss is in a bad humor today—everything I do is wrong!"?

Now let's just turn that statement around: "Everything I do is wrong—the boss is in a bad humor!"

You'll notice that we've used the same words in our statement—but the nature of the problem is certainly changed!

So be sure you really understand what your real problem is before you try to solve it. Try to write it out in ten words or less. Try to write it in several different ways; try even reversing it, as we did with the example. Such practice will help you clarify your thinking about the problem.

2. *Get the facts.* We covered information gathering in Chapter 4. The importance of collecting facts in the process of searching for a problem solution is that sometimes just a good thorough study of the facts will make a solution apparent. If so, you can then forget about the rest of these steps. But if, after you have studied all you can find on the problem, you still don't have a solution . . .

3. *Go after ideas*—but lots of ideas—all you and anyone you can get to help you can think up. Remember, on almost any kind of problem you can think of, there are many *possible* solutions. The only guarantee you have that you will eventually pick the best solution to your problem is by making sure that you have thought of *every* possible solution. And remember, when you are going after ideas, don't let your judgment get in the way. Don't try to evaluate the ideas at the time you get them. Think up your list of ideas first, then at another time go over the list to see which are the good and which are the bad ones.

4. *Use incubation.* Incubation is sometimes referred to as "sleeping on a problem." In actual practice, however, it may be just a matter of breaking away from your work to take a coffee break or a walk to the water cooler. The purpose of incubation is to give your mind a chance to let up on the

problem so that your subconscious can go to work. After all, your conscious mind—the mind you actually try to use and put to work for thinking—is only a small part of the mental powers at your disposal. Back in the memory cells of your mind may be dozens of facts and associations you may have completely forgotten about, and so haven't brought into use on your problem. But they are still there in the subconscious, and it is the purpose of an incubation period—where you just plain get away from the problem—to give them a chance to come out and contribute something. And, needless to say, if an idea does suddenly pop into your mind while you are incubating, write it down and add it to your deliberate idea list.

5. *Evaluate your idea.* So far, everything we've covered has been aimed at helping you compile a list of possible ideas that you can consider in trying to solve your problem. But you have to remember that no collection of ideas, by itself, is worth anything until something is done with them. This means it is now time to turn on your critical power and decide which of your many ideas is probably the best. The process of evaluating ideas is every bit as important to the manager as being sure that he gets the ideas in the first place. There are some specific tips on evaluating ideas in the next chapter on decision making.

But for now, let's say that you have gone through all these steps; you have defined your problem; you have studied up on it; you have developed a list of several possible ways to solve the problem; you have given yourself time for an incubation period; and you have evaluated your ideas and now have what you consider to be a very good idea. What's the next step? It is one that has already been mentioned:

DO something with that idea!

The best idea in the world won't do you, or your company, or anyone else any good at all until and unless something is done with it. Even a fair idea, put to use, may do more good than the most brilliant suggestion no one ever hears about. So when you honestly think you have a good idea, do something with it.

If it concerns a personal problem, and it is under your control, try your idea. If it fails, try another one.

If it is an idea for the company, start the wheels turning to get some action to implement it. Remember, of course, that the people you will be telling about this idea haven't gone through all the mental preparation on it that you have, so be prepared to explain in detail why you think this is a good idea; in other words, be ready to do some selling on it.

If your idea should be one that will involve a patent, check with your lawyer or the company legal department to find out about its patentability.

If it is an idea that you think will help someone else solve a problem they have, by all means *tell* them what it is.

Do *something* with every worthwhile idea!

And don't become discouraged if every idea you produce isn't an instant success. Really creative people always maintain their creative expectancy—they always expect to succeed in solving a problem in the end, no matter how many discouragements come up as they go along.

The manager's prime purpose in being is to make decisions. This includes the knowledge of when to stick by a decision which has been made, as well as when to reverse a decision that is proving out to have been a bad one.

7

Sharpen Your Decision Making Skills

Decision making has always been a popular subject for executive study and analysis. This high degree of attention has already generated enough basic knowledge of ways to evaluate alternatives and plan for contingencies to enable any executive to move his own deciding out of the by-guess-and-by-golly state into something approaching an art.

In this chapter we will consider the next big step in the art: the attempt to further upgrade skills by taking advantage of scientific principles and technologies to sharpen the tools of judgment and knowledge. The basic principles are embodied in an overall concept usually labeled "statistical decision making." Specialists, variously called operations analysts or systems analysts, have been leading the way. Unfortunately, most contemporary accounts of their work get all involved in esoteric mathematical formulas, computer applications, extensive research projects, and the tremendous man-hours that must be spent in fact finding.

Such complexities, while important indeed to the working practitioner of operations or systems analysis, tend to obscure the real significance of the work these men have been doing: the development of a basic concept that can lead to better decisions by anyone.

In an admittedly broad simplification, what the concept means is that decisions are based on significant facts or problem factors which have been given definite values and compared to other facts in their quantified forms. And, without benefit of calculus, electronic computers, or an army of researchers, this is something any executive can learn and begin to apply immediately to improve his own decision making at whatever level of authority he operates.

To settle the statistical aspect of the process, Irwin D. J. Bross, author of *Design for Decision,* points out that "the name Statistical Decision is something of a misnomer. Many people other than statisticians have grappled with the problem of decision and have contributed important ideas. The statisticians arrived on the scene rather late (and more or less accidentally). They translated the existing ideas into statistical terms, added some ideas of their own, and then assembled all of these concepts into an integrated mechanism for making decisions."

Dr. Edward G. Bennion, a leading industrial economist and a mathematician himself, sums up what the manager's attitude can properly be with the observation that "establishing probability coefficients on the economic forecast is a job we can relinquish, more than willingly, to the company economist. We are not concerned with what kind of crystal ball he gazes into, but rather with how top management uses his findings, whatever they may be."

Furthermore, in the modern concept, an executive is not asked to do anything he isn't already doing to some extent. In any decision that is made, the decider goes through the process of developing alternatives and somehow, consciously or unconsciously, of placing relative values on them before he decides in favor of one. Modern executives are also accustomed to using figures and statistics to control their operations. But in the usual operation, executives use the statistics to analyze results, and only secondarily as clues to causes. This is a much different attitude from seeking out the relationships underlying the facts, which is the aim of the statistical concept of decision making. "Putting numbers on the facts" simply forces (and, in many cases, makes possible) more explicit definitions of problems and makes easier the job of selecting the alternatives that may make up part and parcel of the answers.

The Method

Generally speaking a statistical decision involves these steps:

Defining the problem in detail.

Quantifying the factors.

Manipulating the factors to determine relationships.

Weighing relationships to determine the decision.

The beauty of the method is that it can be adapted to any need and carried as far as the user wishes to carry it. This means that it can be every bit as valuable to the retail store operator as to the manufacturing tycoon; it can be applied to personal and domestic problems as readily as to major economic or production situations. The rest of this chapter is a nontechnical introduction to the applications of the concept with generalized methods you can begin to apply to almost any problem you meet up with.

Defining the problem: The heart of all statistical decision making techniques is the specific evaluation of the factors that will be, or could be, involved in a decision. This means you must start out with a specific breakdown of the problem to isolate and define the significant parts, whether they are fixed or variable.

The tendency most people have on facing a recognized problem is to attempt to move immediately to some action on that problem. They jump the step that should come first: analyzing the problem as a guide to what the action must be or should be. And without a specific analysis of the facts in detail, what appears to be a simple decision can turn into a large mistake. One hypothetical example illustrates this:

Jones Manufacturing Company has decided to cut their sales costs in one territory by dropping sales service to one of two marginal customers. Customer A purchased $50,000 worth of products in the 10 years that he has been a customer; Customer B has purchased $40,000 over the last 8 years. Which one should be dropped?

At first glance, it would seem to be a fielder's choice. At second glance, there could be a decision in favor of seniority if sentiment should play a part in this. But actually, with the facts so far in hand, no decision should be made because the facts as stated are not inclusive enough. On probing deeper, we can construct this chart to show the history of sales volume for the two companies:

(dollar sales in thousands)

	1955	1956	1957	1958	1959	1960	1961	1962	1963	1964
A	$1.5	2.5	4	6	6.5	7	7	6	5	4.5
B	$—	—	1	2	3	4	5	7	8.5	9.5

Now we find that there is a difference in the two customers. If we can settle for a simple A or B decision, we are now in position to make it. Cutting off either of those customers will not represent loss of an average $5,000 a year. Customer A would cost Jones Co. less than that and Customer B would cost much more.

The type of thinking which involves taking the second mental step to analyze what is behind the apparent facts is a key to making better decisions.

It is better thinking to think in precise, exact terms: "It will cost us $1,836 next year if we lose that customer," rather than the generality, "It always costs money to lose a customer."

If it is not possible by nature of the problem, or the facts available, to put such exactness into your thinking, you may then want to attempt to apply the more generalized laws of probability. Probability is a complete study in itself, but again in over-simplified definition, it consists of figuring the odds, often in simpler combinations than any good poker player can handle with ease. For example, it is better to say "There are four chances out of five that we will lose Customer X if we don't make immediate deliveries to him nine-tenths of the time" than to say "Customer X won't stay with us if we don't deliver promptly." With the odds spelled out in defining the problem, it is not too much of a step to analyze your past delivery records and determine the probability of being able to hold Customer X with your present system, and if not a favorable forecast, where the trouble will come and what might be done to correct the situation.

Quantifying the factors: The heart of the statistical decision is that once the factors are isolated, they are then given definite numerical values which may reflect either desirability or liability. This is where many business executives turn their backs and begin walking rapidly in the other direction. There are some men who prefer not to commit themselves to an opinion as definitely as is done by placing a numerical value on it. Others just do not want to think that hard. They will argue that many of their problems, particularly those involving people and intangibles, do not lend themselves to specific quantifications. And, in some instances, they are right. At the same time, even the attempt to assign some numerical values, however "boxcar" they may be, will force a thinking through of a problem that, by itself, will probably lead to a more enlightened decision.

It is important also to establish how much accuracy you will really need in a given problem situation. For example, if you just want to know if something can be done, without regard to cost or time, then very rough figures will suffice. On the other hand, if you want to know how well it will work, or exactly how much it will cost, or a precise definition of the probabilities of success, then your facts will have to be qualified more precisely.

It is also completely permissible to hedge your calculations—as long as you realize and admit that you are hedging. For example, the PERT (Program Evaluation Review Technique) system now so popular in the defense production industries provides a reasonably accurate and workable method of scheduling highly complex projects which may often involve the work of several or even dozens of contractors, all of whom have to "come out even" in order to complete a project on time. But even here, in an activity which involves detailed planning to the nth degree, allocating time values to the different activities is usually done on the basis of three separate estimates: the most optimistic; the most likely; and the most pessimistic. In attempting the job of quantifying a number of variables, it is usually easier to do it in two steps: first a rough evaluation where you simply pick out those factors that seem most important, then a refined evaluation where you tighten up and get specific. Here, as an example, is the way it might work out on a personnel assignment problem:

Following is a list of characteristics which are considered desirable for a business executive to have:

Position performance	Creativeness
Intellectual ability	Verbal facility
Human relations skill	Sociability
Technical knowledge	Sensitivity (to people)
Breadth of knowledge	Leadership
Planning	Develops others
Administrative ability	Self-motivated
Efficient work habits	Positive attitude
Quality	Vision
Dependability	Self-control
Acuteness	Initiative
Capacity	Drive
Flexibility	Self-confidence
Analytical ability	Objectivity

Now, imagine that you are a manager considering which of six men to promote to fill a top management vacancy in your company. You have this list before you as a guide in making the decision. Just simple common sense should guide you to the first realization: none of your six men is going to fill all of these requirements equally well. Furthermore, for the job you have in mind, some of the qualities will be more important than others. Therefore your first, or rough, step should probably be to decide just which of these characteristics will be important to some degree for the man who will be selected for the job.

The next step is to assign definite numerical values to those qualities you have selected. On a more refined basis, this could include psychological research and detailed studies of the performances and comparable personality factors of predecessors in the job. And to manipulate the data resulting from these you probably would need a computer. But let's say that you either haven't the time or facilities for such analysis, or else that you just plain don't want to do it. Your next step, then, is to try this:

First, assume that the desirable characteristics you have selected can be purchased in any quantities for 10¢ each. You have $10 to spend. How will you shop for them?—i.e., how much will you spend on each of the characteristics you have said are important?

When you have done this, look over your resulting purchase list. Let's assume you have decided to spend $2.50 on technical knowledge and $1.20 on administrative ability. Now think this through. What you are really saying is that you consider technical knowledge to be twice as important for this job as administrative ability. Do you really mean that? Possibly you do, but one of the prime advantages of quantifying your thoughts is that you have the opportunity of studying often unrelated factors on a common basis. This can only lead to better decision making.

Your next step, on this example, would be to evaluate each of the six men on how well they possess the characteristics you have set up and evaluated. The actual decision, from a purely numerical point of view, will then go in favor of the man whose personality pattern most closely matches what you had previously set up as being ideal. This, of course, will be true only if you have been completely objective and impartial in all your work so far. Also, there may be good and sufficient reasons why something other than personality traits should be considered in this situation. But these can also be factored in the same manner, and even compared against an overall value for personality.

Often a nonmathematician will find he can arrive at satisfactory values by means of what, for lack of a better term, we will call "analogous analysis"—comparing values to other values with which he is intimately familiar. Edwin Miller, of Lincoln Electric Company, gives an example of this in reporting on why his company decided to purchase a new 1,000-ton press:

"We bought this press," he says, "to handle some new products and to accommodate changes in existing products. If we were to buy these new parts outside, the additional storage we'd need would be equivalent to one of our two manufacturing bays. We'd also have to add two people to overhead to maintain the stock. Actually, we can manufacture the parts for about half the cost of buying them outside, use about one-tenth the storage space we would have needed, and make up the parts as we need them."

By thinking in terms of what it would cost to purchase the parts outside, what storage would mean in terms of present manufacturing space, and what additional help would be needed on the payroll, this decision is quickly reduced to pros and cons in simple terms and can be justified as simply.

On more complex problems, you can sometimes program your analysis into simple steps. As an example, consider the problem of assigning sales responsibilities between your sales force and your promotional efforts such as advertising and merchandising. The first step is to determine just which sales tasks must be performed for your company. One relatively common and simple listing looks like this:

Contact new prospects.

Communicate knowledge of the products.

Maintain a favorable attitude toward the company.

Make specific proposals; ask for orders.

Keep customers sold for repeat business.

(See worksheet, page 105)

At this point, assuming that these are the tasks for your company, you can assign some values. This time, assume you have $1 to spend and you can buy any or all of these in any quantity at 10 cents each. List your expenditures in the column headed "Relative importance."

Your next step calls for temporarily ignoring the values you have just developed and considering each of the five stated tasks as a separate whole. Now you assign specific responsibilities to the sales force and to promotion in a total

SALES TASK vs. PROMOTION TOOLS

Sales task	Relative importance of each sales task	Contribution to sales task performance		Net contribution to sales effort	
		Sales force	Advertising and promotion	Sales force	Advertising and promotion
Contact new prospects					
Communicate product knowledge					
Develop and maintain a favorable attitude toward your company					
Make specific proposal and ask for order					
Keep customers sold and get repeat business					
	100%	100% each line		Total	Total

of 100 per cent of each of the five tasks. For example, you may say that you will split the task of contacting new prospects, 50 per cent to the sales force and 50 per cent to advertising and merchandising. At the same time, when you get down to making a specific proposal, you may want to give 100 per cent of this responsibility to the sales force.

Next you combine the percentages to get a numerical value. For example, if you said that 50 per cent of the responsibility for contacting new prospects should be given the sales force, and you originally gave this a value of 20 per cent (or 20 cents) in the total sales task evaluation, then the sales force ends up with 10 on this count. When you have worked this out for all five factors, and for both sales and promotion, add up each column to arrive at a total of what part of the selling job for your company should be the responsibility of sales, and what part should be the responsibility of promotion.

At this point, your worksheet can tell you several things about your own expectations. It can, for example, give you some guidance in determining the budgets for both sales and promotion. It will also give you a quantified listing of what you think your sales force should spend their time doing, and to what degree. And it gives you a listing of objectives for promotion with specific values placed on the importance of each.

Some divisions of General Electric Company use what they refer to as the "worth method" for getting specific values into the process of judging new ideas which may be under consideration. The way it works is this: before any other form of judgment is applied to an idea, the question is first asked, "How much will it be worth to us if the idea can be made to work?"

Once the answer to this is obtained, the next question is, "How much will it cost us to make it work?" Needless to say the answer to this one is not always easy to estimate, but by attempting to do so, the company at least gets a rough picture of the investment and return factors that could be involved in a proposed innovation. A ten dollar idea that would cost fifty dollars to implement is, of course, dropped from further consideration. On the other hand, an idea that could bring in a million dollars a year for several years may get a great deal of further study even if the projected development cost might be a million dollars.

Manipulate the factors: The statistical concept of decision making also allows numbers and their relationships to be a jumping off point for reaching an understanding of an operation.

For instance, on any of the examples already given, assume that you do not agree with the answer provided by the numbers you have developed—you just plain don't like the answer, and don't want to go ahead on the basis seemingly called for. This is, even statistically, the permanent prerogative of the man who must take the final responsibility for a decision. In such a case, you can legally, morally, and with complete confidence begin to juggle the numbers to change the relationships.

Let's say that you have, in one of our examples, given a particular factor a value of 20 per cent. After getting your final answer, you would prefer to make that 30 per cent. Go right ahead—but remember, 100 per cent is 100 per cent, and that other 10 per cent must be taken away from some other factor. It is just like spending money on one of two desirable objects: you may have to settle for less of one, or even give it up entirely in order to purchase the other. With a statistical decision you can make an answer come out any way you want it to just by juggling the values you assign to the factors. But the fact that you are working with specific numbers forces you to do this in a considered manner, with any consequences clearly laid out in full view.

Another advantage is that, when you have a choice of several seemingly equal alternatives, you can test them by comparing numerical scores across a variety of combinations. To test alternatives, you start with any arbitrarily selected combination and "score it out." Then work out your next best common sense option and compare it to the first. If you want, do this with a third choice. Now look for relationships or patterns that might indicate where the sensitive areas are—those parts of the problem most susceptible to improvement if the relationships can be established and/or changed.

This search for patterns can be a valuable aid in making a choice among alternatives. Patterns of some sort exist in nearly every situation. It is the way racing fans pick their bets; the way stock market professionals govern their actions. As Theodore H. Brown, an authority in statistical quality control, points out, "These patterns of experience are to be found everywhere. We say that one person is dependable or that another is erratic. Whenever an individual who was dependable suddenly becomes erratic, some reason is sought for the change."

The key to using patterns is that when you find one that seems to be consistent through a number of alternatives, but does not fit into one or two others, you look for the reason. Here are some quick ways to uncover patterns:

Ordinary graph paper allows you to plot out the numerical values of a series of numbers (whether graphing them would ordinarily make sense or not).

Assembling several series of numbers into line-and-column charts will often make erratic sequences stand out.

Attempting to rank a series of factors—starting with the largest and continuing down to the smallest—will sometimes reveal a surprising amount of information. For example, if you are interested in cutting costs, ranking all your costs will quickly point out the areas where the biggest gains can be made. All too many industrial cost-cutting programs are aimed against what can only be considered marginal expense items, compared to some of the major items that would provide big opportunities.

Adding cumulative percentages to a ranked list of numbers can also be revealing on certain types of problems. An example is analysis by profitability of the accounts of a manufacturer. By putting the most profitable, or largest volume customer, at the top of the list, then ranking other accounts down to the smallest customer, adding cumulative percentages of total business as you go, you get a detailed and comprehensive picture of just where the bulk of income comes from. Match this up with a similar ranking and accumulation of selling costs for different customers, and you see where the bulk of your money is going. Companies who have done this have frequently found that there was such a disparity between the two—sources of income and outlets of income—that they began to wonder how they managed to stay in business.

But through all this manipulating of numerical symbols, you should remember that it is basic to the concept of statistical decision making that a decision be made. The final objective is to clarify the relationships between several courses of action, or between several factors which must be considered in terms of some goal.

The method itself will never make a decision. This act still remains the prerogative and responsibility of the man with the problem. The method will not set objectives; the man must do that. Neither will the method translate an indicated decision into an aggressive course of action. This is also the job of the man. And, in many cases, the decision must be made against the course of action seemingly called for by the indicators the statistics develop.

It is sometimes necessary, for example, to ignore the indicators that a particular market will be ripe for exploitation in ten years provided the company invests heavily in preparing for it now. In this case, it may be necessary to commit resources and manpower to short-term markets for the sake of immediate income—no matter how glittering the long-term prospects may be. And only the manager can make that decision.

What the statistical tools do provide is guidance to the decision maker in terms of giving him a clearer picture of the odds for or against a particular course of action. Therefore, when he does move, he moves with his eyes wide open as to the possible hazards and consequences of whatever action he may take. This is quite different from considering a statistical *approach* to be a foolproof method!

But the man who has probably done more than any other to popularize the concept of statistical analysis, Secretary of Defense Robert McNamara, points out that "You cannot make decisions simply by asking yourself whether something might be nice to have. You have to make a judgment on how much is enough."

8

The successful manager will usually be a master at utilizing time. Time is a tool, along with money, manpower, and resources.

Make Time for Managing

The managing of time for an executive is usually a function of delegation. If an executive has really done the job he is paid to do in developing his staff and assistants, they should be carrying much of the load for his operating responsibilities. This means the manager can concentrate his time on his primary responsibilities: planning, weighing, evaluating.

Many managers are overworked. But there are others whose primary problem is that they do not have enough to do. And even the overworked men occasionally find themselves with unexpected blocks of time when there are no immediate demands to do something specific. There are many reasons for this—all legitimate, and none of which should cause alarm for even the most dedicated efficiency expert. In some businesses there are seasonal factors which can cause voids in the management workload; for example, customer vacation periods or plant shutdowns, seasonal selling or production factors. And, of course, simple circumstances often produce a lull in the needs for active management; i.e., nobody needs the man's help at that particular time.

Such open periods occur at every level in a company—they may actually be more prevalent in the upper echelons where staff support should be taking most operating details off managerial hands. To the individual concerned, such breaks in workloads are often greeted as cause for alarm. Most executives expect to be busy and expect things to keep happening around them. And when a man suddenly finds himself with nothing to do, his first reaction may be akin to shock or disbelief.

Many managers, of course, look forward to such times as "think" periods. These are usually the future-oriented types who respect opportunities to plan and to look ahead. They do not really need any special advice; they can take care of themselves.

There are, however, many men in executive ranks who do not really know how to use such lulls. Their reaction is apt to be that they now have some time to kill. And often a man with time of his own to kill can infect the rest of the corporate body by his seemingly lackadaisical behavior.

In this chapter and the next we will examine opportunities for making time work for you in both areas: first, how to get more time for the vital activity of thinking; and secondly, how to fill the time you make or the occasional lull more productively.

As mentioned, time management for the executive is usually a function of delegation. And delegation, in turn, is a process of developing systems and procedures to handle the routine. Anything that can eliminate detail from supervisory, executive, and administrative loads today is well worth considering. That is why a manager bent on gaining more time for his primary management functions will do well to start by examining his overall policy programs to see if better organization of "housekeeping" details, through use of standard procedures, can help. With fewer details to concern himself with, an executive is then free to concentrate his thinking in more creative and productive directions; he can devote more of his energies to increasing overall company efficiency and well-being.

Standardized procedures must, of course, be tailor-made to the company or organization in which they are to be used. They will usually, however, fall into one of these five categories: product, personnel, production, procurement, or promotion.

These are not in any order of importance, as the relative importance of each will vary from management job to management job. The listing is, furthermore, purposely broad to indicate all possible areas for studying a company's functions.

The best approach to the survey is to first study the list in its entirety in order to get the broad outline of what is included. Then, find those functions closest to your own interests. These you study with the aim of making imaginative transfers of the suggestions to your particular problem. Once you have suitably explored your own primary interest area, and have taken whatever steps and actions seem needed, you can then broaden out into contingent areas—those immediately adjacent to your own function that either affect the way you must perform your job, or that are, in their turn, affected by the way you handle your part of the operation. Like any other checklist, this one is designed to be adapted to a particular situation, rather than adopted as a whole. And, needless to say, the details of studying these areas can be delegated to subordinates.

Your Product

Too often, when a new product or service is standardized to the point of full production, it is then forgotten by everyone other than the actual people who have to turn out *x* number of units a week and the sales department who are required to sell those units. However, nearly any company will benefit from a policy of examining products both at the time they are launched for full-scale marketing, and then at regular, fixed periods for as long as that product is on the market. Some of the points such a policy should cover are these:

Ways to increase production. Is full utilization being made of present production facilities? Would simple modifications of system, procedure, or flow enable us to increase production? Are we using the latest known methods for handling all operations?

Ways to decrease costs. In this area a company should have fixed policies to accomplish two things: first, to make sure that if costly expedients were resorted to in the heat of getting the product ready for market, a search is made for different ways of accomplishing the same function. As an example, a company producing an electronic component used several tuning knobs on the control panel. In order to get the knobs they needed originally, they turned them out in their own plant at a cost of $2.25 each. Once in production, however, they had time to look around among their suppliers. This search uncovered a plastics manufacturer who agreed to produce the knobs for 25 cents each.

The second point a cost reduction policy should cover is that of making sure that new methods of manufacture, or new components, or new materials do not come onto the market without being tested or measured against those currently in use. As a general rule, most products should be reexamined every six months for possibilities to cut manufacturing costs either through methods or materials substitutions or changes.

Ways to improve quality. Most production or service departments require reports of customer complaints and product rejections and repairs. A standing policy may be possible to provide for regular study of complaints by designers as a means of pinpointing chronic product weaknesses that might give competitive products a marketing edge. The objective is to eliminate those surprises that cause the panics that require management time to settle.

Standardization of design and components specifications. The usual pattern of company growth is one of expansion into related products, or, as in the case of a consumer product like toothpaste, of expansion into self-competing lines in an attempt to garner a larger share of the available market. In either case, product B is apt to bear some similarity, either in make-up, production requirements, or marketing needs to product A which preceded it. Product C, which follows B into production, will, in turn, carry over some similarity to B. These similarities, of course, offer many possibilities to standardize either minor designs or major components. In this case a standard policy can save endless hours of meetings, conferences, and bickering which will be expended if every product must be treated as an individual group of separate problems.

Materials testing. In order to protect itself and its position in the closely competitive markets we have now, a company should have a detailed policy to provide for a materials testing function: who will do it, how it will be done, what standard tests will be run where there are standards, and who will be responsible for devising new tests if necessary and what, exactly, should be the objective in testing.

Utilization of stock parts. In order to enjoy the economies of purchasing commercially available stock parts, there should be a company policy spelling out just how far to go in using stock parts as product components. This may be based on the considerations of a competitive situation; i.e., could a competitive edge be gained by some exclusive or patented part? Or it may be dictated by the need to provide a unit which can be readily serviced by anyone anywhere. As an example, when Minnesota Mining and Manufacturing Company introduced a new machine for applying plastic tape to metal pipes as a corrosion insulator, they designed the taper entirely from commerically available, or readily fabricated, parts. This machine is intended to be used anywhere anyone might want to coat pipe—in the field beside a ditch as well as in a plant or yard. Therefore, it seemed desirable to make it as easy to service and repair as possible. 3M was primarily interested in selling the tape used by the machine, so there was no real reason to design in any special "exclusives." Such marketing considerations can be valuable as guides in deciding just how far you want to go in use of stock parts. And it can save much expensive design time if your designers have a "road map" showing just which route you want them to follow on given types of projects.

Your Personnel

In spite of the attention that has been paid to industrial and personnel relations in the last few years, there are few companies so progressive that they still don't have some blind spots in personnel relationships. Here are a few places where policies may have been overlooked:

Organization structure and functions. Does your organizational structure take into account the future growth needs of your company? Some companies have traced back their growth patterns and found a correlation between personnel and sales figures. This gives them a formula for predicting future needs in nearly all their job classifications. These companies also set up their organization structures to allow for orderly expansion of functions, departments, and subsidiaries along the lines of their predicted growths.

Job classifications. This includes job descriptions. It is, of course, necessary to assign responsibilities and authority in a business structure, but, at the same time, it is possible to make a job compartment too tight. If workers, or executives, are so restricted by their job specifications that they are never exposed to problems or problem solutions from other jobs or departments in the company, their ability to grow as individuals may be severely handicapped. In fact, there are personnel specialists who feel that overorganization may be the real villain in our present shortage of generalists.

Personnel records. Personnel records should be much more than just tax records. Functional records that include previous job skills, special training, hobbies, outside interests, educational and geographic backgrounds can do much for a company when extra or emergency help is needed for special problems. Complete personnel records, which are also completely available to anyone who may need a particular skill or background at any time, are a first step in organizing for maximum personnel utilization.

Discharges and layoffs. Every employee, whether an hourly worker or an executive, has a right to know where he stands in regard to discharge and layoff policies. Even unions agree that certain abuses merit immediate dismissal or a penalty layoff. The trouble usually starts when someone attempts an on-the-spot formulation of a new policy for an offense never before considered punishable, or where the punishment has often been bypassed for one reason or another. Any absolute reasons for either discharge or penalty should be spelled out to everyone in such a way that they cannot possibly be misunderstood. These should cover such general categories as personal behavior, health, and production cutbacks, as well as performance and quality standards.

Accident prevention. Here are some questions that can be asked, the answers to which may provide guideposts for measuring or improving your safety program: What is your cost per year chargeable to accidents? Include hospital charges, compensation insurance, damage awards, wages paid during incapacitation, and production losses. What accidents are more serious in nature? Which are temporary? Where do most accidents occur? Are particular types of accidents highly recurrent? An important part of any successful accident prevention program is the maintaining of up-to-date and detailed accident records, with an automatic policy of attention in the event anything gets out of the ordinary. And, as long as things are running well, let them run.

Job instructions. Any employee should know at all times and under all circumstances what constitutes a job instruction. If it is policy to issue detailed written instructions for all work, then the employee should not be expected to take a sudden verbal change at full face value. On the other hand, if, as is more usual, it is common practice to supplement written instructions with verbal, the worker should know exactly who it is that has the authority to make verbal exceptions or changes in what he has in writing.

Your Production

Generally, production policies cover the actual plant and physical equipment needed to produce a product, and the utilization of that equipment to maximum efficiency.

Equipment inventories. Is sufficient equipment on hand to meet all production demands? On the other hand, is equipment inventory overstocked? Is there idle equipment a significant part of the time? Could special-purpose equipment be rented for short-term needs? Could time on other manufacturers' equipment be borrowed or rented to do small-lot specialized jobs? By pinning down the policies on questions like these, the responsible executive can eliminate endless disruptions and interruptions while he tailor-makes endless individual decisions.

Performance specifications. Production cannot be planned for maximum utilization of equipment without adequate information as to what a machine can do under varying conditions. For example, a milling machine will have different rates of production on aluminum, brass, and steel. In a plant with many machines of a type, the efficiencies of the various operators will have to be taken into account, or even averaged out, to make reasonable predictions of production abilities. In either case, there is no substitute for detailed analytical records to help the production men, and the policy should be to see that such records are made and regularly analyzed, with the analysis converted to usable form.

Maintenance. Policies here should cover details of repairs, replacements, and obsolescence, with specific responsibility assignments for policing these details. In some cases, responsibilities will include either the machine operator, regular plant maintenance crews, or special members of the engineering section. Often all three groups will be—or should be—involved. When you assign out such responsibilities, you can't be too detailed if you want your maintenance effective.

Tools and fixtures. Toolmaking and fixture usage should come under the policymaker's eye in the realm of establishing standards for judging when to make them, and when to purchase a nonstandardized unit. Possibilities to standardize tools and production fixtures should also be looked into. Frequently, a slight redesigning of a part will in no way impair either its function or its efficiency, but will make it possible to utilize existing tools or equipment in its production.

Materials handling. Materials handling, including storage of raw materials and semi- and fully-processed products, is often a stepchild in the full production picture. Storage space and warehousing is often space that is not needed for anything else, or space that happened to be the cheapest available at the time it was first needed. Thereafter, it was a habit. In considering materials handling as a policy target, it is important to ask "Who?" in connection with most operations. Frequently, the responsibility for moving or storing supplies, materials, parts, or finished products actually bears no relationship whatever to the most efficient handling methods or the most convenient storage locations for smooth production flow.

Quality control. As a general rule, you can "begin at the end" in your search for the places where manufacturing quality control standards should be applied. By starting with the end product, and working back through the steps leading up to it, you will undoubtedly find places where an insistence on higher standards at the preceding step will result in either a better finished product, or a less expensive step in producing the product. Either way, it will mean fewer management headaches if recurrent problems can be eliminated.

Your Procurement

Procurement in the average company includes a combination of the usual purchasing function with that of designing and specifying the items to be purchased.

Centralized versus decentralized purchasing. This will depend to a large extent on the type of operation a company is engaged in. If purchasing requirements are relatively simple, chances are the most streamlined handling will be through a single department. As purchasing requirements get more complex, however, a single unit may prove inadequate. In which case, considerations should be given to decentralizing the function. For example, a dollar value limitation may be set, below which individual units may do their own buying for day-to-day needs. Anything over this limit must go through channels. An obvious pitfall to watch for is that of duplication of many small orders for common supplies which, if purchased in quantity, could be bought more cheaply.

Another formula for decentralizing the purchasing function is based on types of materials. As an illustration, the purchase of new materials, to be used in limited quantities for research or pilot plant production, may often be made the province of the unit or department needing those materials. The pitfall here is that once a purchasing authority, however limited, is given away, there may be some reluctance to give it back even after the original reasons for the assignment are no longer valid.

A third formula for decentralizing is based on stock levels

and usages of materials. Those materials for small-quantity short-term needs, i.e., today or tomorrow, are ordered by the person needing them at the time they are needed. Long-range needs, which are more predictable, are purchased through a central unit. A possible pitfall is the human proclivity to overestimate the urgency of a situation, which can lead to both extravagance and subquality buying.

Single source versus multiple sources of supply. Most purchasing men are advocates of the multiple source of supply, as a hedge against ever "getting stuck" due to the internal troubles of any one supplier. Most materials and component manufacturers, on the other hand, would like to get all the exclusive business they can from a company, and will put up lengthy arguments and cite case histories showing how their customers have always been protected on deliveries. There is actually much to be said for both sides on this question and the final policy for any company will have to be based on their specific needs and past experiences. One point that should be clearly resolved, however, concerns the economies of single source buying: Some larger and broadly diversified suppliers have adopted policies whereby quantity discounts apply on the dollar volume of the order, rather than a quantity basis. This makes it possible for a customer to order many different types of supplies from the same company and enjoy the benefits of quantity discounting over the whole order.

Planning and purchasing coordination. It is all too common for a design group, with sales, marketing, and other such planning functions, to carry a new product right up to the point of production, and then call in the purchasing man to tell him what is needed in the way of supplies, materials, equipment, tools, etc. In enough cases to have significance, had the purchasing man been made a member of the planning team, he could have made valuable suggestions along the way concerning availabilities of standardized parts, alternate materials or components, and ways to save having special parts made. It should probably be a policy that no product leaves the design department in the first place without a review by a competent purchasing specialist for possibilities of cost-saving. This might eliminate the need for those frequent cost-cutting hunts which consume so much executive time. It is often doubtful that the savings which finally accrue weren't more expensive to achieve than the original extravagances!

Your Promotion

One of the chief distinctions between the way business is done in the United States, and the way it is done in most other countries, lies in the American exploitation of promotional possibilities. Yet even some of the most promotional-minded American companies frequently have many loose ends in their operation which, if properly tied off, would result not only in smoother operations demanding less managerial supervision, but would also give them important benefits in more effective promotions.

Marketing responsibilities. Basically, the marketing concept which has been getting so much attention lately simply means starting with the consumer in your product planning. In other words, you start with what the people you expect to purchase your product want, or need, or think they want or need, and then tailor the product to those people. But many companies are still trying to sort out the details of who is to interpret these needs, or how their old products can be tailored to the new marketing concept idea, or how they can promote old products under the new rules. Both sales and advertising departments are in the act, and in some companies, there are now new marketing departments sandwiched in between. Where these departments are assigned a coordinating role, they can function very effectively. But some of them are only serving to confuse the issues and divide the responsibilities for any real planning. Therefore, one of the first promotion areas to be looked at must be the fixing of responsibilities for determining the sales, advertising, and/or marketing strategies a company will employ.

Budget allocations. One generally accepted way of determining promotional budgets is to put allocations on some fixed basis such as percentage of sales, or percentage of sales plus anticipated or desired increases. Another method to consider, particularly when introducing a new product, or opening up a new market, is the task method. This starts with an estimate of what it is the company wants to accomplish, and then, working back, establishes the price tag to accomplish the task. Though this is not particularly compatible with long-range planning, a switch can always be made to a percentage of sales when conditions warrant it. But from a policy standpoint, it is far better to have a uniform method of determining how to allocate promotional dollars rather than an annual or semiannual guessing game.

Agency liaison. Another place where many advertisers waste motion and money is in their advertising agency relationships. Agencies, on the whole, are equipped to perform a dual function for the advertiser client: act as marketing and selling consultants by virtue of their widely diversified experience in the specialist business of advertising and also act as purchasing agents for publication space, TV and radio time, and outdoor display facilities. They provide, of course, the necessary creative and mechanical skills needed to bring an advertising campaign into being. However, an agency, to be most effective, must be allowed some latitude in professional recommendations, and be given a certain amount of confidence and security in making their recommendations. Agencies frequently claim they are handicapped by too many cooks in the client kitchen—people with the power and influence to direct, or misdirect, the advertising expenditure or content, but who are not, at the same time, available to the agency for preliminary planning or for explanations to support particular recommendations. Therefore, one of the first places to begin to improve your advertising agency relationships is to carefully define, in policy form, just how the agency will operate, and with whom it will operate in the company.

Reviews and appraisals. Although there are many shortcomings in the various measurement tools, it is possible, within reasonable limits, to measure the effectiveness of advertising and other promotional efforts. A sound policy is that of periodically—quarterly or semiannually—reviewing promotional efforts by means of whatever methods of measurement are available: readership ratings, inquiries produced, impact scores, sales leads, and even, when possible, actual sales produced by each specific promotional item. And, as all these are past records, it would be in the nature of insurance to set aside a certain percentage of each annual allocation for pretesting advertisements and campaigns on which you are going to spend the bulk of your money. There is nothing to beat soundly documented success stories on past promotional expenditures to save the promotion man time in getting future budgets approved!

In summary, probably any manager looking at all the issues raised by this checklist en masse, could be forgiven for any misgivings he might feel. However, as stated earlier, this is intended to be a broad survey of possibilities, and you shouldn't even begin to think of capitalizing all these possibilities at once. You start where you are, in any way you can. As one astute administrator observed, "Overhauling a company is a case of becoming a patchwork specialist. You patch here, and you patch there, and finally the patches become a new shell, and the changes are all made."

It would also be a mistake to hold off doing anything until you have the perfect package all wrapped, ribboned, and tagged. If you can start anywhere in getting any company operations into a standardized policy form, by all means do it. If you wait for perfection, chances are you will wait forever.

And finally, remember that policies are not panaceas.

Blind adherence to any policy can result in new thinking being frozen out. So be sure to examine any policies you set up regularly in the light of current conditions. Better still, if you can do it, build in automatic feedbacks for your policies that will let you know when an exception should be made, or when it is time to change. But when it comes to saving time, there are few techniques as effective as having standing policies to cover the routine, backed up by an organization that understands the policies and can execute them with a minimum of managerial supervision.

For the manager time is the one tool that cannot be replaced if it is wasted. The good manager will not, therefore, let it be squandered or dissipated.

9

Use Thinking Time for Thinking

When a man is productively busy, he usually manages by one means or another to concentrate on the parts of his job that are most important—where the results will be most significant. Less demanding details and the minutiae of running the business are delegated to others. With time to spare, however, the man's guard is apt to go down. Out of sheer boredom (or loneliness!) he may let himself get wrapped up in operating details and less productive pursuits, such as being father confessor to the malcontents and chronic complainers in the organization. Instead of using his time for building or planning, the man finds himself handling noncritical details and special, but also noncritical, requests just to have something to do. So the first rule for making productive use of thinking time is *beware of trivia.*

It is the nature of business that the higher a man rises, the greater is his responsibility for the productivity of the work of every person, including himself, under his personal control. Rather than regress to detail or trivia himself, the executive should use his time to study his organization. It is usually difficult to properly evaluate any activity when that activity is being done under pressure. It is equally difficult to objectively evaluate subordinates or staff personnel when you are dependent on them to keep the wheels turning in critical times. It is difficult, if not impossible, to plan long-range courses of action when TODAY is the critical time you must live through.

But thinking time should be the time for a manager to stand back and look at his organization and his people. He has the opportunity to study to learn what is important, or significant, or even missing. And he has the time to apply imagination to foresee and anticipate future problems before they can happen—even, perhaps, before they can become problems. But these important opportunities are lost if, simply because nothing apparently more important is happening, the executive lets himself get trapped by the trivia that is always awaiting the unwary manager. A manager relaxed should be a manager still. What he does is trade off managing the present in favor of managing the future.

One thing to keep in mind is that an ever-present danger to the manager with time on his hands is that he may develop a feeling of frustration or uselessness. This is particularly true if the quiet period is prolonged for any length of time. The average manager in American business got where he is by being a producer, a man of action and accomplishment. He is used to the creative satisfaction of a challenge well-met; a series of difficult assignments well handled. When he is suddenly taken out of action for any length of time, his imagination, far from being an aid and help, can become his enemy. In an effort to make himself feel useful again, he is tempted to channel his energies into almost any activity that will give him some sense of purpose and accomplishment in return for the outlay of effort. And no matter how enlightened the man may be on the importance of planning, such intellectual exercises seldom give the feeling of accomplishment that actually concluding some successful action brings. So the second rule for effective use of thinking time is *relate your effort to your responsibilities.*

Men who aren't realizing a full sense of satisfaction from their work can often be spotted by excessive availability for business "socializing"; or numerous plant inspection trips; or sudden departures on speaking trips "for the company"; or overentanglements in civic or community affairs—all of which can make the man unavailable for company needs when he is again needed. In moderation, of course, none of these activities is bad—in fact, to some degree, all of them should be requisites for a responsible executive. But we are concerned with the excesses which are the signs and symptoms of a man without enough to do and who doesn't realize that slack time can still be productive if it is used productively.

It is possible that the man himself lacks definable and recognizable goals. Without personal goals, he may also be unconscious of his own responsibility to set management goals for the company. Rather than use his unloaded time to examine present operations with a view toward setting realistic goals for future performance, he is apt to let his own operations and organization drift as he himself is drifting. The time he is killing with nonproductive pursuits is time he should be devoting to developing objectives and intermediate milestones; finding ways to measure values of operations and chart progress; and of finding and developing new opportunities for future growth toward significant objectives.

Without well-planned goals, both individuals and organizations quickly go adrift in a sea of indecision. The executive must discipline himself to look ahead—to search for the trends and indications; to develop the relationships between company capabilities and the future to keep either the company or his own limited responsibility moving in a straight line toward a specific goal. Plant tours are important—but they should be planned for a purpose. Business socializing is important—but it should be done with an objective in mind. Representing the company through speaking engagements and community activities is important—but only as they are really related to the good of the company. Any executive who remembers to relate his activities directly to company goals has no reason ever to feel useless. Time productively spent in building for the future is never killed—it is an investment in future business life.

Executives with time on their hands, whatever the reason, should automatically start looking for ways of streamlining methods; of speeding communications; of gaining greater efficiency in day-to-day operations. This is done by starting with a study of things as they are; what will be required to reach objectives; and what is missing between the two. The manager can then determine and fix responsibilities definitely and clearly. He is then free to bring his own authority to bear to encourage the use of imagination and positive action to achieve the desired results. This brings us to the third rule for using thinking time: *Have a plan.*

Here is a checklist of thirty-six areas which should be legitimate concerns to every management-level executive.

Each offers unlimited opportunity for improvement and progress, and all can be spare time activities for any executive.

Study the Future

1. What significant research is being conducted in your company?...in your industry?...by your suppliers? What changes will be required in products, methods, or techniques if and when the research pays off? What *plans* will be needed to make it pay off?
2. What are the economic trends in your industry?... in your plant's community?...in your state? How will these affect your business 1 year from now?...5 years from now?...10 years from now?
3. What shifts can you foresee in your labor situation 3 years from now?...in 5 years?...in 10 years?
4. What impact will electronic data processing or automatic production equipment make on your organization?... in economics of operations?...in labor?...in methods? ...in needs for special executive skills?
5. What will you have to do differently in your organization 3 years from now?
6. What new products will you be able to offer customers 2 years from now?
7. What new prospects will be available to your company in 3 years?...in 5 years?...in 10 years?
8. What can you do now to be ready for efficient entry into the new markets of 1970?

Study Your Organization

9. What has been the growth pattern of your employment in sales?...research?...production?...administration?

10. For each of the last ten years, are there any clear-cut relationships between the number of persons employed in your company, or any of its specific functions, and the dollar sales volume?...the units of production?...the number of customers served?

11. Do any of the above point out significant areas of study for the future?

12. Do they reveal opportunities for improvements in the present? For example, how do your competitors compare on these counts?

13. How is the efficiency of the sales department measured? ...the research laboratory?...the production line?... the shipping department?

14. Are work measurement standards for either individuals or departments realistic? If not, why not?

15. Will your present work measurement methods be capable of handling your problems in 1970?...1975?... 1978?

16. What areas of your present organization are not now subject to work measurement? Why? What method could be developed to apply objective measurements to all organizational performances?

17. Try this test: circulate a "buck slip" memo or bulletin

to five individuals through regular company mail channels. How long does it take to get back to you?

18. How long does it take to answer a letter from a prospect who has requested price information?

19. How long does it take to answer an inquiry resulting from advertising?

20. How long does it take to get a credit report on a new prospect?

21. Try this test: call your own sales department from an outside phone with a vague request for information on one of your products and without requesting any specific individual. How long did it take before you reached a qualified person who could handle your inquiry? Would an impatient customer wait that long for the information?

22. What other problem areas can you uncover in your internal communications? How could they be improved ... specifically?

Study Your People

23. What methods of work value measurement are in use at the hourly worker level? ... at the foreman level? ... at the executive level? Are these consistent? If not, what are the inconsistencies?

24. How do you, personally, measure the value of work performed by your subordinates?

25. Can you give a numerical efficiency rating to your three immediate key subordinates? If yes, how could they

be raised to 95 per cent? If no, what factors would enable you to develop such a rating?

26. What ways are in use in your company to measure or evaluate the development progress of various individuals? Are these consistent? ... realistic? Will they still be adequate in 1970?

27. What plans have you for developing or acquiring the management skills your company will need in 1968? ... in 1973?

28. Which (and how many) of your people would require retraining if your company made a complete change to electronic data processing in three years?

29. Which of your staff functions are most active in charting the future concepts for growth of your company? Is the activity commensurate with accomplishment?

Study Your Methods

30. Rank all your overhead expenses (rent, light, heat, fixed salaries, etc.) in descending order beginning with the single largest dollar amount. Which items are you now putting cost reduction efforts against? Are these the ones with greatest potentials for savings?

31. How old is your oldest piece of regular production equipment? Are any of your competitors using newer equipment for the same purpose? If so, do they enjoy any competitive advantage because of this?

32. How are costs of operations (including staff and administrative) figured? Are the methods realistic?

33. Do all your administrative costs represent actual contributions to the value of your product or service?

34. How many procedures or systems do you have that have not been changed in the last 12 months? Are the original conditions that caused the procedure to be established all still the same?

35. What procedures or methods seem to have the greatest inefficiencies in them? Can they be simplified? Can they be eliminated?

36. How many people receive a typical internal memo or bulletin which you issue? What is your justification for each person on the list?

Time to spare...time to kill...unbusyness...unloaded hours—these are all times of choice; to grow or to stagnate, whether the manager is thinking of himself or of his company.

There is no lack of opportunity to use uncommitted time productively.

The manager must know people in general —their capabilities, weaknesses, aptitudes, drives, and motivations. It does not mean he must like people. But he must understand them.

10

Learn to Use the Tensions That Motivate

There is a growing conviction among many management analysts that businessmen may have gone overboard with the cult of what is usually defined as the human relations school of management.

Executives have been barraged with advice on understanding their workers' deeper feelings and needs for satisfaction. One well-known business speaker even has a "commandment" for bosses to the effect that they shall "love" people.

Under company sponsorships, employee reading racks are filled with such pamphlets and tracts as "How to Get More Fun Out of Your Job," "How to Get Along with Your Boss," "How to Work with Others," and so forth. The fact that such pieces disappear from the racks somehow—and an occasional employee is seen reading one during an otherwise solitary lunch break—is taken as evidence that the "messages" are getting through.

The general idea of all this is that every company should be a happy, smooth-running ship, free of both tensions in the individual workers or the organizational conflicts that create them.

There have always been, of course, some bosses who refused to go along with this line, but, in the past, they were usually brushed off as old-fashioned fuddy-duddies, out of tune with today's social enlightenment. But serious inquiries are now being made into just how foolish such "reactionary" types really are.

147

When profits are declining and growth rates level off, the men responsible for running major companies can be excused for beginning to wonder if perhaps we haven't gone overboard on the happy ship idea, and perhaps what is needed are a few more good honest tensions and conflicts to stir things up somewhat.

Even respected psychiatrists are publicly voicing doubts that it may be foolish to suppose that you can make every aspect or detail of a man's job either enjoyable or interesting. One recently admitted that there are times when it is probably better to appeal to the fighting impulse in a man for certain jobs. His suggestions included that of making a man feel ashamed of being frightened by a particularly tough customer or prospect—rather a change from the advice businessmen have been hearing that such a situation calls for an understanding attitude.

There is also a growing reacquaintance with an old principle of psychology that affirms that sometimes you can get a man to go at a particularly tough assignment with what William James described as "an inner wrath that is one of his best moral faculties." And, as James pointed out, "a victory scored under such conditions becomes a turning point of his character."

Much of the propagation of the tension-free climate theory has come about in management development clinics, programs, and institutes. These started out to supply more or less formal education for executives and bosses. For this objective, such efforts had a definite place and value. But when, in a few hours, or even days, they attempted to develop new attitudes and habits on the part of executives, they were only partially successful. And, in the psychology of handling people, as in so many other subjects, the little knowledge that remained after brief and intensive exposures often proved to be dangerous to the welfare of the companies sponsoring it. The advocates of tensionless and conflict-free organizations either shortchanged or completely overlooked some rather basic fundamentals in human behavior. Or at least their students haven't always remembered them in trying to apply the teachings.

The first is that civilization and progress stem from discontent. When man became tired of pulling loads against maximum friction, he invented the wheel. When he became completely dissatisfied with the fickleness of dame nature in supplying his needs, he was driven to invent irrigation, fertilizers, plows, and other such aids to replenishing his food supplies. When his power wants outran the abilities of animals, his dissatisfaction led him to invent engines.

Another basic is that the nucleus of human motivations still consists of the motivations of childhood. No matter how sophisticated an adult may become, beneath the surface are the attitudes and motivations he had as a child.

Basic to childhood motivations are the forces based on hostilities. People try to love each other, but they seldom succeed. Every person, it is true, desires love and recognition in some form. But, as Dr. Leon J. Saul points out in *Bases of Human Behavior,* the average person meets with far less love than rivalry, envy, greed, and hostility. This is readily built up into feelings that one is consciously disliked by others, is discriminated against, and so on.

Another fundamental reality was touched on by Ernest Havemann. Writing in *Life* magazine, he described modern American man in his office world as occupying "a lonely and precarious niche between unapproachable superiors and timid underlings around which rivals circle like vultures on reconnaissance."

Recognition of such overlooked fundamentals as these, plus a few more of primary interest only to psychiatrists, led to a meeting of mental health people in 1960 to study the whole problem of just how far business and society should go in trying to eliminate tensions and conflict-producing situations for the good of mankind. Out of this meeting, the first of many, there is now appearing the growing school of psychologists who are willing to bet that there is little a boss can do to change all the members of his staff into living bundles of outgoing corporate joy through work, cooperation, and job satisfaction. There is, they feel, little that can be done within the job context to erase the basic human traits of worrying, inferiority, ill temper, and resentment which each of us carry bottled up inside ourselves.

These scholars are now suggesting that the boss may be much better advised to stop trying to be father confessor, guiding light, friendly physician, and old buddy to his workers and concentrate on being the boss. Since, they conclude, there is not much that he, the boss, can do to change his workers in their basic instincts anyway, the best approach he can take is that of using those instincts for the best interest of the business.

Recent industrial studies tend to confirm the opinions of this new class of psychologists. These studies show that high morale among workers does not necessarily mean high production, and the old-fashoned "tyrannical" boss often gets better results than his soft-spoken public-relations minded son who has been listening to the lectures.

Under the circumstances of some of this new evidence, today's executive may be much better advised to begin listening to such prophets of human behavior as Dr. Ralph W. Gerard, professor of neurophysiology of the University of Michigan, who claims that a little anxiety is good for a man. Among the benefits of tension, claims Dr. Gerard, is that it brings into use brain cells otherwise inactive; it heightens attention, improves performance, and facilitates learning by a greater spread of nerve messages in the brain.

And psychologist Dr. Harry Johnson, writing in *The Saturday Evening Post,* has said: "Not all tension is bad. A homespun fiction character named David Harum once observed that 'a reasonable number of fleas is good fer a dog— keeps him from broodin' over being a dog.' Tensions in a human being," says Dr. Johnson, "are something like fleas in a dog's life. A reasonable number of them, although they may not prevent a man from brooding over his membership in the human race, do provide interest and excitement and keep him scratching for an upper bracket income. They are a spur to ambition, achievement, and happiness."

Ernest Havemann also quoted a psychologist who said, "When I'm in an airplane, I don't want my pilot to be some slaphappy, easygoing bundle of joy who's too busy laughing and relating to the stewardess to worry about the instruments. I prefer a tense, rigid man who's so loaded down with obsessions and compulsions that he can't take his eyes off the dials. If I'm lying on the operating table, I'm not interested in knowing that my surgeon is a nice fellow with a lot of empathy for his nurses. For all I care, his nurses can hate him—as long as he knows what he's doing and has them on their toes."

Certainly any manager can set up parallel examples in his own company—particularly if he has just come through a quarterly meeting with his board of directors and a less-than-satisfactory profit and loss statement to explain away. Under such circumstances, he is apt to wonder if it is, indeed, so important to have a happy crew and "satisfying" climate, or if perhaps there isn't something to the theory that the boss should be the boss and use any moral means at his disposal to get his organization's performance record up. And any means can often mean the deliberate, willful, and premeditated use of personal conflicts that will lead to tensions and a revival of the flight or fight instinct.

It is a medical fact that if a person is under stress, say anxiety, he reacts to it physiologically. An example is the increased pulse rate in a student before an examination, or in a speaker before he takes the podium. These are common signs of the body's preparedness under the stimulus of tension.

Emotional conflicts can easily lead to the drive to satisfy

those conflicts. Every executive has had the experience of hiring a young, single man fresh out of high school or college who approaches his job with a certain casualness and exhibits disinterest, not only toward the work, but even more toward the idea of getting ahead in the company. But before long, the young man falls in love, marries the girl, and is on his way to the financial responsibilities of being a homeowner and parent. Suddenly his apathy disappears and he becomes a veritable tiger toward his job. His ambition seemingly knows no end, and under the stimulus of an occasional raise in salary, his ability grows rapidly. Such a drive, of course, stems from the conflict between his domestic needs or wants and his present income. And the reverse correlation shows up as he approaches his late thirties and early forties when his immediate financial needs have been met, and his income and living habits have settled more or less into balance. With the conflict removed, his tensions and, consequently, his drive, begin to let down.

Further evidence of the concrete value of conflict is found in studies conducted by psychologist Bluma W. Zeigarnik. She gave a large number of students a group of twenty puzzles and similar problems to solve. They were allowed to work on half the problems until completed; in the second half they were interrupted before they could finish. When the students were later asked to recall as many of the problems as possible, they remembered considerably more of the unfinished ones. Dr. Zeigarnik concluded that unfinished tasks leave a tension or dissatisfaction because of a desire to solve the problem which is frustrated. Hence, students remembered them better than the complete tasks where tensions were relieved.

Other than the sex drive, the main goals of men can probably be generalized as self-respect, respect of others, health, and material gain. The proponents of the benevolent boss and organization have always supported the theory that the motivations for these should be of the pleasurable type. But even Freud pointed out that the desire to gain pleasure was balanced by the desire to avoid pain. And it is in the second part of this principle that the value of tensions and the conflicts which cause them should be examined by the boss who feels that his people are capable of more and should do more.

There are, of course, known methods of creating tension in an individual and in an organization. There are also excesses to be avoided. In applying these forces, the manager will have to avoid several pitfalls which will be taken up later.

Two general types of conflicts can be initiated: those which work to build tensions and stimulate drive in individuals, and those which work to motivate an entire organization. For each conflict, there is a caution—often more than one. But by a judicious balancing of conflicts and cautions, new life can often be put into tired people—or companies.

The first type of conflict which comes to mind, and the one most easy for a superior to create, but, at the same time, the last one he should probably ever use, is the threat to a man's livelihood—the threat of firing. This is put first in the list of deliberate emotional conflicts not as a primary recommendation, but merely to get it out of the way. It is, as stated, the last a boss should use. Threatening to fire a man amounts to an ultimatum, and one should never use an ultimatum of any kind unless he is ready to be called and have it picked up. It is not the intention of the boss who seeks to stimulate and energize his people to have them quit on him. Quite the contrary. What he should be applying are the stimulants that arouse his people to action for the good of the company. And these can be a good deal less drastic than the threat to fire.

There is, for example, the simple deadline. Who among us hasn't had the experience of having the boss, or a big customer, drop a normal three-hour job on his desk one hour before he had planned to leave the office to play a round of golf, or attend a long-anticipated dinner party or some other activity considered highly desirable? And because the strength of the desire was strong enough, the man was able to get the three-hour task accomplished in the hour that remained.

Firm and fixed deadlines for the completion of work have many advantages to offer. First of all, they do get a man's emotions involved in the task—and if planned right, they will present a real challenge. They also rule out the very human trait of procrastinating when an assignment is open-ended so far as time is concerned.

An alternative to an individual deadline is to broadcast a schedule of activities to be completed with specific completion dates. This act alone can set in motion a series of interrelated conflicts involving performance standards, competition, and challenge. It can also be a means, in itself, to coordinate activities through a range of subjects. Deadlines are a very useful form of conflict when you want to generate emotional involvement in completing a task. Assigning a job without such a target date for completion is like being asked by a friend to "come over for dinner sometime." The very indefiniteness of the invitation provokes a feeling of insincerity and unimportance.

Another source of beneficial conflict lies in the performance standards you establish when assigning a task. There is no stimulus to a man if he is asked to, or allowed to, work below his capabilites. Many of the standards we find ourselves accepting in others actually do fall below their true abilities. They have fallen into habit patterns and habitually fall back on their past methods and personal standards in measuring their own performances. And what becomes habit in another person, can easily become the expected for those around him.

In such a situation, a tension-producing conflict in the form of a sudden new expectation of superior performance can often jolt a person out of his lethargy. The initial hike in known expectations shouldn't be too great, of course, but it should be enough to let the man know that previous methods and performances won't be quite good enough for this job—he will have to reach a little higher. And on subsequent jobs, he should continue to be pushed until high standards become his new and accepted habit pattern.

William James, a pioneer psychologist and expert on habits and how to make and break them, advocated this progressive substitution of new standards for old on a continually challenging basis in teaching people how to acquire new and more desirable habits. As a case in point, he cited the "fatigue pattern" most of us follow in our daily lives. According to James, if we are used to finishing our workday at 5 P.M., we are also used to the idea that we should be tired at the end of the working day. We become so used to this, in fact, that we are apt to leave our offices feeling exhausted. The technique he advocated to overcome this was to progressively push back this fatigue point by mentally extending the day. This was accomplished by gradually extending the work stopping hour a little more each day until his subjects could frequently manage ten or more hours without tiring and without loss of efficiency.

Another stimulus which can conflict with a man's past habit patterns is that of setting a quota for alternatives to be suggested on a given problem. The aim here is to stimulate a man to greater than habitual resourcefulness. Chances are, if you have a subordinate who can usually suggest two or three good ways in which a problem might be solved, even such a modest challenge as asking him to produce five alternatives for your consideration will force him to extend his own resources. To meet this quota, he will have to reach out beyond his habitual avenues of thought, and will also, in all probability, have to include other people in his search for solutions. This type of a conflict challenge is of particular value if you suspect a person of playing his job too close to the vest and not communicating freely enough with the people he is supposed to work with.

A pitfall here is to be certain you don't again set the standards too high initially. If a person can usually produce two or three alternatives to a problem, you would run the risk of complete frustration and hostility if you suddenly confronted him with a quota for ten. This is changing a mental hurdle which he can be expected to leap with a little extra effort into a positive barrier which he can probably not surmount with even a killing effort.

A conflict built around alternatives and ideas is also that of challenging for positive thinking. This opportunity frequently presents itself in meetings, conferences, or even private discussions with the negative type personalities who often seem to be waiting for someone else to make a mistake so they can pounce on it.

The technique, in this instance, is to simply ask someone who comments negatively on a proposal to come up with a positive alternative. If you do it often enough, and insist on compliance, one of two things will occur: either the negative type thinker will be jolted out of his destructive habit and turn into a more constructive contributor, or he will at least develop a healthy respect for those who are willing to make constructive suggestions and be more willing to consider their ideas from a positive viewpoint.

The organization chart offers another opportunity for creating beneficial conflicts. Too often, as mentioned earlier, in attempting to chart responsibilities and authority in a company, the tendency is to make the job compartments as specific and tight as possible. Lines of authority and communication must be defined in any large organization, of course, but if, at the same time, the idea of lines of opportunity can also be incorporated, the organization as a whole can often benefit greatly.

"Lines of opportunity" refers to the machinery whereby any interested party on the same level of authority, or within a level or two, is allowed to take an interest in what others are doing though it may not be within his specific specialty or responsibility.

The net effect of this is that everyone, up to and including the president, knows that someone else may be looking over his shoulder with the perfect right to make suggestions at any time. This will usually bring out the competitive urge in even the mildest tempered executive. It is also practically a guarantee that a supervisor will stay on his toes. No executive can afford to be completely complacent and rest supinely on his laurels when he knows an ambitious subordinate is free to come after his job at any time and all he has to do to get it is show he can produce.

This is not, however, an argument for divided responsibilities, or failure to delegate responsibilities specifically. In fact, specific definition of responsibility is one tool that can pay off in almost any management situation.

The specific and public delegation of a responsibility by itself introduces a conflict situation. To the man who receives such a publicly delegated assignment, it means that from then on he is performing in a goldfish bowl; and he cannot ignore staff or other contributing services when they ask for instructions, or when they desire to contribute inputs. Also, he knows that everyone else knows that the responsibility for failure, if any, is his.

Furthermore, this is a definite step which must be taken

on any project in order to insure complete communications. This was discovered the hard way by a manager who had just finished briefing his staff on a major project they were to undertake. Walking back to his own office from the conference room he overheard one of his subordinates say to another, "Well, who has the ball on this one?" This was, of course, a clear sign that no one in the group felt in any way responsible for doing the job of investigation and organization that would be necessary to complete the project. The easiest way to prevent this is, again, to make one man definitely responsible, or assign individual and specific responsibilities to the individual staff men.

Personality chemistry also offers an opportunity to introduce beneficial conflicts into organizational tasks. Too often, in setting up a team or group to handle a particular problem, the manager leans over backwards to try to select people who will "get along together." But there are times when a little friction will actually generate competitive pressures, or even complimentary tensions, to get results far faster than teaming men who get lost in enjoying each other's personalities.

In highly generalized description, there are three basic types of personalities to consider in a team "mix": the mental types, who are predominantly intellectual in their approach to problems and situations; the emotive types, who tend to let their feelings predominate in their actions; and the vital types—those who prefer physical action to any other type of activity. There is, of course, a little bit of each of these in every person. Furthermore, it is a mistake to "type" a person permanently because the dominant characteristics may change from time to time or situation to situation depending on the stimulus of the moment. However, the executive with an appreciation of human chemistry can often set up teams or groups that will generate spontaneous action in response to a given problem—and make sparks fly to the benefit of all concerned.

Another way in which modern managers are beginning to differ with the "humanitarians" of recent years is in the general demeanor of the boss himself. It has been a popular theme over the last few years that the boss should avoid giving direct orders and should attempt, through psychological machinations of one kind or another, to persuade people to do the jobs they are being paid to do. Consequently, many executives have adopted the policy of asking "Do you think you could get this out for me?"... or "Would you take care of this when you have a chance?" or some such softly worded request. However, today's managers who have been experimenting with direct orders are finding to their pleasure that the direct instruction to "Get this out by this afternoon" or "Here is something I want you to take care of today" is infinitely more productive in making things happen than worrying about the psyches of their high-paid executives.

A similar rule of humanitarian management that is being tested and found wanting is that of how far the boss should go in taking advice from subordinates on the feasibility of projects of various types. The past advice has suggested that if the boss made a request for an action, and subordinates reported back to him that for any of a number of reasons the action was not a good possibility at that time, the boss must give serious consideration to this advice. This was considered the "democratic" way to manage.

However, in checking the backgrounds of such negative recommendations, managers have often found that "can't be done" reports often reflect either laziness or lack of resourcefulness of the subordinate making the recommendation. Or, even more subtly, it is done by the subordinate just to get a reaction out of the boss to find out how important he really did consider the assignment. This, in a way, amounts to testing the boss by presenting him with a conflict between what he thinks could be important or valuable to the company, and the negative reaction of his staff.

Needless to say, no manager can afford to ignore completely the negative recommendations given him on projects. Neither, however, does he have to immediately back-track on his request and accept a "can't be done" report without further probing and questioning. By being slow to accept reasons why projects should not be carried through, the manager will set up a conflict situation that can easily result in getting more of his ideas carried out to positive conclusions.

A somewhat related conflict situation can be created with an occasional and deliberate crash program. In spite of the pentagon wag who described crash programs as "getting nine women pregnant in order to make a baby in one month," they do have a place and a value. The place is when the majority of questions on a problem have been resolved, and the lines of action clearly defined. The value is that of crystallizing action for the sake of accomplishment. The crash program is another means of bringing out the competitive urge that exists in most individuals by setting up the requirement for a series of coordinated and interrelated activities to be carried out simultaneously and with minimum procrastination. If one person lets down, everyone knows it; the challenges are explicit.

Each of the conflict situations outlined here has in it the idea of setting a goal—either attaining a certain performance standard; or meeting a given deadline; or completing a task with the responsibility assigned to it; or making oneself live and work efficiently with other personalities with whom the man himself may not be entirely sympathetic. Each such situation will set up minor tensions which have a chance of bringing out better performance from the man put into the conflict situation.

However, as in any goal setting, the manager applying the conflict principle should be sure that in setting goals the goals are attainable. Don't generate frustration in your quest for stimulation.

Tension, also, must be watched once it has been generated. Tension can quickly build itself into anxiety—and here, perhaps, the "humanitarians" do have some advice worth following: in the midst of a difficult or complex or discouraging assignment, every man can use a word of encouragement from the boss. This is particularly valuable when you are deliberately trying to build tension in order to attain a goal. The fact that the boss stops by to say "You're doing fine—keep it up" can be the difference between the worker continuing to work under pressure and enjoying it, and his becoming discouraged and embittered by his "unreasonable" boss.

Another pitfall, for example, would be to continue trying to build tensions indefinitely. Such stimulations work best when they are used occasionally—to jolt minds out of the ruts they may be in, or to awaken them to new opportunities. But it is again a psychological principle that if danger and fear continue indefinitely, the human organism tends to adapt in some way—to find some form of equilibrium. The arousal to fight or flight begins to quiet down. Still another psychological principle at work is one called homeostasis—the tendency to adapt. Constantly being kept in a state of tension can have the effect on a person of making that the new norm. Complacency begins with "Ho-hum—another hot assignment." This, of course, is self-defeating.

But the idea that every worker has to enjoy every phase of his work, that he should be allowed, like water, to seek his own level of accomplishment, just doesn't jibe with what is known about the successful business leaders of the past or of today. These men demanded and demand performance. They do not worry about whether their subordinates are well adjusted or free of tensions. In fact, most of them agree completely with Harry Truman's advice:

"If you can't stand the heat, get out of the kitchen."

The manager must be apt at delegation. There is an absolute limit to the amount of work even the most willing person can do. Once that limit is passed, there must be a division of labor; the work must be spread around.

11

Build Your Delegating Skills

Most managers give at least lip service to the popular reasons for delegating: to free their own time for important planning and to develop the people under them.

Utilizing others to carry the burden of operational work details is accepted as something that should be a constant aim for an executive. In fact, in an American Management Association Workshop Seminar on "Top Management Planning and Control" it was recommended that the president of a company should spend only about one per cent of his time working on today's problems; two per cent working on problems a week in advance; and up to 30 per cent of his time on problems in a time frame of 3 to 4 years distant. Even a department manager, according to AMA, should spend only about 10 per cent (half a day a week!) of his time worrying about today's problems; 10 per cent thinking about next week; and as much as 39 per cent thinking about problems 3 to 6 months in advance. But few presidents and still fewer department heads ever achieve so idealistic an apportionment of thinking time. Both are usually much too busy just minding the store for today or tomorrow to have much long-range planning time available. Yet plans are vital to the orderly growth and development of any business, and the task of obtaining such planning time is a basic objective of delegation.

The developmental benefits of giving others responsibilities are not to be ignored either. An executive has a dual responsibility to his company in regard to subordinates: he must first be sure that he is getting capacity work from each man; and, secondly, that his own replacement will be ready at such a time as the executive himself either moves up or leaves the firm. The manager who does not delegate runs the risk of having his people work far below their true capacities; and he also risks having his more ambitious and capable subordinates leave in search of greener pastures as soon as they have obtained what valuable experience they can—thus depriving the company of the benefits of that experience.

These are, of course, the standard textbook reasons given for executives to delegate. Many managers, however, have read the manuals and textbooks and have only succeeded in reaching the conclusion that their writers have never had executive responsibilities themselves. If they had, the managers feel, they wouldn't be so quick to advocate delegation as the royal road to managerial success—not when there may be extremely costly or risky projects to be completed against urgent deadlines. When the chips really are down, "letting go of the reins" isn't usually as simple and easy as the advisers make it sound. And this is often even more true in medium- and smaller-sized businesses.

True and complete delegation to someone else is often about the most difficult thing an executive in a smaller company ever has to do. It means he must be willing to allow others to make mistakes with what is often his own money. More than that, he has to actually encourage them to run the risk of making mistakes and then charge those mistakes off to the experience of another person.

Delegation, basically, means to trust another to act for

you. Because it involves trust, it also involves the risk of trust misplaced. And when any executive who has delegated a trust to another finds out that matters have gotten out of hand, it doesn't make too much difference that the mistake was unintentional or that the assignment was not clearly spelled out. His first reaction is that the other man fell down on the job and he has been left exposed and defenseless before his own superiors. This is also a risk of delegation: the buck stops at the manager's desk. He cannot delegate the final responsibility for a failure.

The National Management Association has listed more specific reasons why executives, down to and including foremen, fail to delegate: "Lack of confidence in subordinates' abilities to learn ... unwillingness to pay the price of training subordinates ... fear of losing recognition and prestige ... unwillingness to trust details to others ... the lack of desire to see subordinates grow and prosper ... a feeling that the modern worker is unwilling to accept authority and responsibility ... a belief that hourly workers cannot possess authority to make decisions."

Popular as these beliefs are, they cannot really be considered more than excuses for not delegating—they certainly do not measure up as reasons. After all, it is an inescapable truth of business that if the people in the organization never made mistakes, never forgot or overlooked anything, never got into each other's hair, there wouldn't be any need for managers, superintendents, department heads, or foremen. A business would run itself quite well without the supervisory overhead.

The pros and cons of delegating probably net down to

this: the executive, to be an executive, must delegate. His primary responsibility is always to the company. And if his company has given him assistants, it is because he is expected to produce more in the way of accomplishment than he can supply by himself. He has the responsibility of utilizing his subordinates. His delegation, however, should be planned, controlled, definite and clear if it is to be as effective as it can be. In other words, it is as important how you delegate as it is that you do it. And the first step to take is to define the goals.

The first goal of delegation is to achieve the position of management. When an executive does a job or performs a function himself, he is not managing. Managing is planning the job and getting it done, not doing it yourself.

The second goal is to develop the people under you to make them more capable and effective. Any manager is ultimately judged by the people he develops because only through such development can the continuity of a business be assured.

The next step is to consider just what delegation really is—and what it is not. One definition is that "delegation is having other people do part of your work." This, however, is inadequate because you can usually accomplish that without really delegating. A better definition, favored by the NMA, is "giving others the right to make your decisions." Still another is "to give authority to accompany responsibility." This latter is an accepted maxim in almost every treatise on delegation. It is also probably much more honored in the breach than in the keeping. Many executives who are liberal in parceling out responsibility, often sincerely believing that this is delegating, negate the possible benefits by keeping the real authority in their own hands.

Of these three definitions, the one that comes closest to fitting both the spirit and intent of real delegation is "giving others the right to make your decisions." This is also the one that usually proves to be most difficult for a manager to accept.

"How," he will ask, "can I give others the right to do what I am paid to do? This is, after all, the essential difference between my job and that of my assistants—I am expected and paid to take the risks and responsibilities of making decisions. They are not."

While this may be true for the overall executive position, any large decision is usually made up of many smaller ones. Any large operation consists of many secondary and detail operations. And this is the key to determining what and how much to delegate.

The executive must analyze his own job and break it down into small enough fragments so that the decision-making can be apportioned out among his subordinates. In this manner, the requirements for decision-making can be commensurate with both the responsibilities to be expected and the general level of abilities found at varying levels beneath the delegating executive. The basic principle involved is that of delegation in depth.

This principle calls for close attention to be paid to the selection of the people to whom you will delegate key responsibilities and give the authority to act in your name. The essential matter for analysis is to determine the nature of the decisions and actions involved in the managerial job, and then match those as closely as possible to the types of personalities available to take them on. This can be a prime pitfall in an unplanned delegation program. As the National Industrial Conference Board has pointed out: "Programs for developing men are being found in countless businesses, but relatively few companies have given serious attention to the prior matter of selection. The cart has been put before the horse."

Another pitfall in this area is to follow a constant policy of playing it safe. This consists of limiting opportunities to accept new responsibilities only to those who are well known as being able to carry them out. It is better to rotate responsibilities, both by size and by type, among all the people available until you have carefully defined the limits of each person's ability under different circumstances. The general rule should be to expect success in such an assignment until you actually are let down. Then attempt to analyze the failure and learn from it.

One reason many executives have gone sour on the whole idea of delegating is that they have, at some time in the past, tried it but at the wrong time. The time to delegate is before you have to. Too often if an executive has the time to do a job himself he does it. But there always comes a time when he himself is pressed for time. By then it is usually too late to teach someone else what is wanted.

In applying the principle of delegating in depth, it is also important not to delegate too high. The person who is actually doing a job is usually the best person to whom to give such a responsibility. In other words, the delegation should be to the lowest level at which the job can be done.

This, of course, raises some questions which must be answered. For example, how do you know such a person is qualified to take on the responsibility? Chances are, if you have analyzed the nature of the task to be delegated, and have correctly picked the level at which responsible action can be taken, the person occupying that position will have the ability and talent to take on the job or he wouldn't have been hired in the first place. It's a mistake for an executive in the act of delegating some of his decision-making power to try to minimize the risk by setting the requirements and qualifications higher than they need be.

It is also easy to fail to distinguish between those qualifications that are essential for a man to have before he starts a job, and those that he can acquire quickly and safely once he has started on a task. The tighter you draw your initial specifications for a man to whom you will be willing to delegate responsibility, the more likely you are to have to compromise on your final selection. As Gifford K. Johnson, president of Ling-Temco-Vought Corp., points out: "You'd be surprised how many different individuals can handle the same job well."

The question also arises as to whether lower echelons of authority have the information needed to see the "big picture" and make their functions contribute to the overall whole. The answer to this is that higher authority must, in the process of delegation, see that sufficient information accompanies the task, and that any necessary continuing information be continuously supplied. This may include such operational items as cost control figures, progress control, and parallel reports for other operations involved in the overall function.

Still another consideration in delegating to the lowest possible level is the problem of having to work through an intermediate supervisor. No top man on the managerial ladder can ever afford to bypass his assistants if he wants to maintain a disciplined organization. Skipping over a supervisor to deal directly with a man under him nullifies the supervisor's authority for that particular function. This doesn't have to occur very often before it will become impossible for the supervisor to supervise. An assistant who is short-circuited out of the chain of command cannot retain the respect or control of his workers when these people feel they can deal directly with the big boss any time they want. It is, therefore, both wiser and sounder to do the delegating through the secondary supervisor if it is necessary to reach an operating level for most effective execution of a responsibility.

This can usually be accomplished easily if the top man enlists the aid of the second-line supervisor early in the problem. It may, in fact, be the quickest way for the boss to locate the actual worker who can take over responsibility for a particular phase of decision making. It is a relatively simple exercise in human relations for the boss to ask a department or section head for details of how an operation is conducted; who conducts it; and then ask for the supervisor's suggestions as to how it might be conducted better. At the appropriate time, the boss can suggest that the specific worker be called in for his views on how the action might best be implemented. Usually, both the worker and his supervisor will be found willing to volunteer to take on a responsibility that will keep work moving. If not, a simple question from the boss along the lines of "Well, who do you think is the best person to see that this job actually gets done?" will usually trigger the answer the boss had in mind when he first began the conference.

Frequently, of course, the boss may find that either the supervisor or the worker will come up with a better idea than he himself had. In this case, it is a smart manager who recognizes the idea and gives some praise for it immediately. This, of course, is one of the key characteristics of the leader: he must be able not only to welcome the ideas of others, but also to plant his own ideas in their minds and to compliment them on their ingenuity.

Working through the second-line supervisor to accomplish a depth delegation offers an added advantage in that it will make the supervisor himself conscious of the value of delegating. All workers in a company usually look to the top man for examples that they may follow, as well as for excuses for their own shortcomings. The boss who sets favorable standards of conduct and management can expect this ultimately to be reflected in the work of those under him. Failure to set the standards—in this case, failing to delegate as much as possible—will also result in a follow-the-leader philosophy on the part of subordinate supervisors.

This brings up another key to successful delegation: under any circumstances the boss must take the time and have any necessary degree of patience to communicate his wants completely. When an executive assigns a part of his job to another person, that person has a right to know exactly what is expected of him. He should know what the boss himself thinks the job should be and what he expects in the way of performance from the worker who is accepting the delegation. The scope of authority should be clearly defined and the man should know exactly what decisions he is expected to make and how much authority has been vested in him to make those decisions. Only in this way does the man have the freedom to go ahead, and only with a specific charter can he be held accountable for specific results.

Such a policy of specific delegation works as much for the boss's protection as the worker's. It is only human to expect a man's ambition to grow with the taste of success, and a worker unused to authority and responsibility might be tempted to exceed the limits of authority which the boss intended him to have.

Then, too, a job can change the nature of a man as much as a man can change the nature of a job. This, of course, is one of the basic reasons behind advocating that the boss delegate some of his authority: even limited exercise of authority will cause the decision-making ability to grow. The precautionary consideration is that once a man does begin to develop and grow in ability, it will be necessary for the boss to keep the channels for growth open and the opportunities ready to feed the ambition that will come with growth.

Another communication problem that must be handled is that of letting other people who will be affected by your delegation know about it. Merely telling a subordinate or line worker that you want him to take over a decision-making function will not, automatically, give him the authority he needs to act in the eyes of those who have been accustomed to coming to you for such authority. The decision-making prerogative must be definitely and publicly conveyed by you or your man won't have a chance.

Communication must also be two-way. There must be a feedback channel through which the person who accepts your decision-making authority can get back to you. You should know every time a critical operation has been successfully passed. You should be informed, in advance, of expected trouble, and immediately when it is unexpected. Properly speaking, if you have really delegated and mean it, the news that something has come unstuck should be accompanied by the information as to what is being done about it. Your job, then, is to review the action, approve, modify, or change it on the basis of your more extensive experience and familiarity with the larger picture. This situation, of building in operational feedback, is summed up clearly by one manager: "When I put somebody under me in business for himself, I always make it a point to tell him that the one thing I do not like is a surprise. He knows he has as much freedom as he needs, but he will be in big trouble if he ever surprises me—even with something good!"

Taking all the possible pitfalls into consideration, together with the initial added burden of implementing a large-scale policy of delegating, a manager can reasonably be expected to wonder whether the game is worth the candle. However there are still other advantages to be derived from a firm policy of delegating in depth. For example, daily operating decisions should not be occupying the manager's time. If he delegates and trains in depth, such decisions should not reach him. And the necessity of constantly checking and double checking other people's decisions should eliminate itself. If responsibilities have been delegated to the proper levels, the operating people at those levels should be checking each other. All these contribute to the ultimate benefit of giving the manager more time to manage.

In spite of these obvious advantages to the manager, some still hesitate to ask others to take on more responsibilities because the other people are considered to be working up to capacity at the present. However, delegating the right to make an operating decision can frequently give a busy man more time. It will often be quicker for him to make his own decision and initiate his own action than to locate the manager, wait until he can be seen, and then wait again until the manager can assimilate the problem and arrive at a suitable decision.

The final expectation is one that will only be appreciated

by managers who have succeeded in the application of the principle of delegating in depth; a realization that there is actually more enthusiasm for their jobs among lower level employees who have been given the opportunity of obtaining the satisfactions that come with successful handling of responsibilities.

The manager must be adept at motivating others to want to solve problems. And his motivation must be of a high enough level to cause others to want to do their best—rather than just to do the job.

12

Make Others Want to Solve Problems

It is basic to any executive position that the man occupying it be able to get problems solved. Not necessarily to solve them himself, but get them solved through the people he has available to work at solving them. In other words, he must know the principles of getting his people interested enough in his problems that they will do the jobs they are to do. We have already covered some ways to do this: create tension that will motivate; use depth delegation. This chapter deals with the positive forces of motivation—leadership techniques that make a person *want* to solve problems because the boss has made the problem interesting.

Ideally, the manager with a problem would always be able to search out the one person who was best qualified to handle that particular type of problem, and who would be most interested in seeing it solved. But this ideal is seldom realized. As Robert N. McMurry points out, "You cannot assume (as a formal organization chart does) that you are starting anew to create an ideal organization made up of ideal people. You must start with what already exists and do whatever is necessary and possible in order to improve it."

"Whatever is necessary" frequently turns out to be the acceptance that what workers in general are most interested in are themselves. Their own problems are of much greater importance, their own wants are of much higher priority, their own interests are much more interesting than any of the problems, wants, and interests of the company.

What about using money as a spur? This is the motivation most managements think of first when they consider extra incentives at all. We read and hear so much about impressive monetary rewards for ideas or special accomplishments that we tend to forget there are other ways to inspire and lead people into extending their capabilities. And the managers who limit their considerations to money only are usually bewildered when they hear stories of other companies such as the Polaroid Corporation where, it has been reported, many employees cannot even guess what their exact salaries are—other than the fact that they are "adequate." In Polaroid, Edwin Land has built a company where the principal spur to accomplishment is individual pride and personal responsibility. The monetary rewards do come to the individual workers, but they are definitely secondary to the interest in the job itself so far as worker motivations are concerned.

This is a practical demonstration of what Elmo Roper, the public opinion specialist, found over the course of a ten-year study of people and their job relationships. He found that the desire for more money ranked fifth in the list of primary job expectations—after job security, advancement opportunity, treatment as a human being, and prestige. Since this was an extremely comprehensive study, cutting across a decade in time, thousands of individuals, and all levels of responsibility and authority in companies of every type, its confidence level should be high enough to indicate quite definitely that workers want and expect more from their jobs than just money.

There are, in fact, several spurs other than money that can be basic in attempting to motivate people: fame, self-realization, prestige, happiness, self-satisfaction—to name but a few. In each case, if a man is susceptible to a desire for one of these, this desire can be transmuted into an opportunity for realization in connection with a specific problem. Let's consider these one at a time.

Fame: This can be as simple as giving a man public credit when credit is due. A common company attitude is: "We are all a team, and the team should get the credit." This is patently nonsense. Any team is made up of individuals, and the contributions of a team come from the individuals on it. The selfish attitude of refusing to credit individuals for worthwhile accomplishments can only result in resentment, quarrels, squabbles, and loss of interest in either the team or the company goals.

Self-realization: "What, exactly, is an achievement?" asks Bernard Haldane. And he answers the question this way: "It is something which you enjoyed doing well and which gave you a feeling of pride. It stirred your emotions, gave you a lift. You'd like to repeat it frequently—in fact, the oftener the better." This points up the key factor in utilizing the spur of self-realization—the fact that a person who has realized an accomplishment is left with the desire to repeat the experience.

Prestige: Though closely related to fame, prestige is, at the same time, distinct enough to merit separate consideration. Fame indicates public or widespread knowledge of a man and his accomplishments. Prestige indicates more: a respect for the man at some level where such respect is important to him. This may be a peer group of people on his own level in the company, or it may be the fact that top management knows and respects him and his work and lets him know of their respect.

Happiness: This is closely akin to the theory that a job should be enjoyable. However, as we covered earlier, no job is enjoyable all the time and in all aspects. At the same time, an individual can find happiness in the successful conclusion of even an undesirable work assignment. And happiness in work seems to be a characteristic of those men who are noted for accomplishment in every field—industry, commerce, the sciences and the arts.

Self-satisfaction: No emotion is so strong as that of the knowledge that a difficult responsibility has been satisfactorily concluded. And every time such a conclusion is reached, the man experiencing the accomplishment grows a little and is that much farther along in preparation for even more challenging tasks. The opportunity to experience such self-satisfaction is a powerful emotional stimulus.

The deliberate use of such spurs calls, of course, for one additional step in the executive's planning process: the thinking through of the method of presentation of a problem prior to giving it to someone to work on. And this, of course, means that planning per se must be more than mere scheduling.

In the chapter on creating tension, we covered the fact that significant accomplishment in any field usually occurs when some individual becomes either intensely irritated or intensely interested by a problem. It is possible to deliberately irritate a person about something to the point where he will motivate himself to take some corrective action. In general, however, the spur of interest is one that is much easier to manage and, more importantly, to control.

Here, then, is where things begin to come together: The executive must first analyze his problem to determine its requirements. Next, he must put what he knows about his people and their motivations against this. Then he must find a way to match the requirements of the two. Harold Geneen, President of International Telephone & Telegraph, summed it up this way: "It isn't any blinding stroke of genius. That's hogwash. It's a thousand little things you have to know and do. You have to work. You have to get information before you can solve the problems. You can't delegate anything if you don't understand it. You can't meet objectives if you don't understand them."

Furthermore, from the standpoint of getting greater creativity from your people, creative authorities are generally agreed that in the main, the most creative ideas come from people who are most interested in the problems. Interest seems to be the one common denominator that distinguishes outstanding innovators from run-of-the-mill problem solvers.

There are, in general, three basic types of problems that an executive has to contend with:

The "old" problem that has been around for some time.

The problem of introducing something new into the work situation.

The problem of obtaining some change in an existing situation.

Each of these has special requirements in attempting to build interest on the part of the people who are asked to solve them.

The old problem: Nearly every company has some problems that have been around awhile. Periodically, or sporadically, management decides another attempt should be made to solve one of these. Now they have a new problem: that of getting someone interested in one more try at something that is well-known as an "unsolvable." As a matter of fact, in some companies it is common practice to reserve this type of problem for new men—on the theory that a fresh viewpoint might yield results that more experienced people haven't been able to obtain. At the same time, the feeling which is never expressed is that such problems offer opportunities to test the mettle of a new man.

But the situation exists: this is a problem with a history of failures in attempts to solve it. How do you interest someone else in trying it again?

The first principle is to realize that not all problems are really opportunities—in spite of the positive thinking cult that says you should always look at them as such. Some problems must be solved out of sheer necessity. And though solving them may reward the individual person who was able to do so, the chances are that neither he nor the company is going to think of them as opportunistic during the course of his efforts. Some examples: Lockheed's problems with the Electra aircraft. At the time they were taking their

$121-million licking, it is doubtful if anyone could have been convinced that this problem represented an opportunity. And it is certain that Ford did not feel their experience of losing over $200 million on the Edsel was opportunity. The airlines of this country may feel that their best opportunity for survival lies in mergers or consolidations, but this is doubtful opportunity at best, because if they could accomplish profitable operations otherwise, most of them would prefer to continue as individual companies enjoying their own autonomies.

The important thing to remember in an old problem situation is to be positive in presenting it to another person. Don't go into the whole horrible history of how long the problem has been around, detail all the failures that are a part of that history, and then expect the recipient of all this agony to perk up and look at this as a personal challenge and opportunity. All you can possibly do with such an approach is to set up a series of mental blocks that no amount of later encouragement can overcome.

There are people who debate this philosophy. They feel that when you put a man on a problem you should give him as much of the background as possible in order to avoid "wheel spinning" and waste motion through covering the same ground that has already been shown to be fruitless. One consultant has a rather unique way of answering this argument. He suggests to anyone voicing this feeling that they try a little experiment. "For the next thirty seconds," he says, "you think about anything you want to think about. Let your mind go free. Think about any subject that comes to you. But don't," he adds, "think about polar bears. Anything but polar bears." This usually results in first a look of concerned concentration, then chagrin, and finally enlightenment as the subject discovers his mind has had a dead short circuit implanted in it.

"Now," explains the consultant, "you can see what happens when you give a man the negative side of a problem. Even though you tell him to ignore or forget the mistakes of the past, what you have really done is to lock his mind onto those mistakes so he cannot get away from them."

The important point in favor of letting a man who is new to a problem cover ground that has been covered before is that, though he may travel the same route as some predecessor, he may get a different view of things along the way. Or he may react to them in different ways. Out of these differences may come a different approach or possible solution that just might solve the problem.

Introducing something new: This is the type of problem, more than any other, where advance planning is absolutely necessary. People do not resist change as much as they resist the idea that they are going to be forced to change whether they like it or not. Any basic change in methods, systems, production equipment, or even new product models that will involve new manufacturing methods, calls for changes in behavior on the part of the people involved. And this will be the chief source of the problems originating in people unless the situation is handled carefully.

Many such problems are forced on companies by their customers. The company is left with no option other than losing the business if it can't accomplish the changes. Therefore, they have to be made efficiently and effectively. Hilliard Paige, of General Electric's Missile and Space Vehicle Division, describes the situation in changing the technology of the space industry: "With ballistic missiles," he says, "our equipment had to last 25 minutes—the length of time of a ballistic trajectory. This time was stepped up to three or four days with the first generation of satellites, like the Discoverer. Now the requirement is switching to a year or more—and our equipment has to last all that time. It costs about $10 million to put a satellite into orbit—and the customer who buys ten of them likes to be sure that they are going to work. They have to last or we are dead!"

In a situation where your problem involves gaining rapid and wholehearted acceptance of something new, the key lies in obtaining the cooperation of workers before it is necessary for them to experience the changes they will be called on to make. There are several specific steps that can be taken to change potential resistance into an active interest in making the changes work.

First, you can solicit ideas for making the change from the people who will be involved in it—even line production workers—in the initial planning stages. This gives them a stake in the problem and, more importantly, a stake in the success of the new method. The caution here is that your solicitation of ideas and suggestions must be sincere: workers must know that you really do want their ideas, and they must eventually see evidence that their ideas were seriously considered and employed where possible. Those ideas that were not used should be identified and reasons given why they were not used.

Another good technique when introducing something new, particularly in the areas of systems, procedures, and methods, is to present the new proposal as an experiment. In this case, the explanation usually runs along the lines of, "Here is something that has been working quite well for ABC and XYZ Companies; let's see if we can somehow adapt it and make it work for us."

The use of announced experimentation is a generally underestimated technique for enlisting cooperation. As long as you present something new as experimental, you have all the freedom you need to make mistakes, to back off and try new approaches, and to solicit advice without seeming not to know what you are doing. Furthermore, if the average worker is told what is going on, he will usually be more interested in helping you reach a successful conclusion to your experiment than he might be in helping you make a success of an arbitrarily imposed new method.

It is important, though, that no matter how you introduce a new innovation, you shouldn't push too hard—or at least, try to avoid the appearance of pushing. People will respond to change if you can first make them interested in seeing it succeed; but they will resist it on principle if they think they are being forced into it.

Changing a situation: Problems that involve changing an existing situation differ from those where the objective is to announce something new in that the necessity for change must first be spelled out, and acceptance of the necessity gained before any progress can be made.

A basic of problems of this type is that not all of them, even those that do include some real opportunities, are going to be fun to solve. Some will be absolute drudgery; some will be emotionally undesirable. It is doubtful, for example, if any manager or group of managers ever enjoyed making the decision to close down a plant and deprive hundreds or thousands of people of their livelihoods. It is doubtful, too, that any manager ever enjoyed having to make the decision to commit a company's entire resources to supporting an entry into a new and unknown market where the risk could have been as much as the entire company's resources. Yet these are problems that must often be faced and must be solved in any business to some degree or another.

There are times, however, when a complete change to something new may actually be easier to sell than a partial change which will result only in a better way of doing something that is already being done. The reason is that in attempting to present something new in an established method, you first have to overcome the feeling most people have that the established way is probably good enough. There never seems to be a feeling of urgency about making minor changes in present methods—even when it can conclusively be shown that making a change would result in immediate benefit.

You can hint, suggest, and mildly question the appropriateness of a particular course of action, or choice of action, that is being pursued. Very often, however, such common techniques of seeding dissatisfaction fail to take root. This is where you have to drop back on the basic motivations that make people go. Try to present the problem in such a way that the person will take a personal interest in it. This can be done through what one master salesman calls "painting a picture of how things could be."

How do you paint such a picture? By appealing to the basic spurs that pertain to the particular person you would like the action from. For example, if he is a man to whom the opportunity for prestige will be a big factor, discuss your desired objective in terms of the challenge of accomplishing it and the respect that awaits the man who can solve the problem. If, on the other hand, it is self-realization that makes a particular man want to perform, your approach can actually be to suggest the opportunity to accomplish a really difficult task.

One caution to keep in mind when suggesting any modification of the way something is being done at present is that the person to whom you are making the suggestion may have been a very big part of the present unsatisfactory situation. In fact, he could easily be the cause of it. This can throw quite a burden on your diplomatic abilities—particularly if that other person happens to be your superior!

In this situation it may not be the best approach in the world to begin to harp on how badly things are going right now. Far better to paint the picture of how they could be in the future—particularly if only one little element in the overall situation could be changed. It may be that there is more than one element that needs changing, but in a situation where you have to deal with a person who may be the basic cause of the problem, it is usually easier to settle for making your gains in small pieces. But here again, knowing what that particular person's basic emotions and drives are can help you find the proper way of presenting your suggestion or request so that you will obtain favorable interest.

Everything so far has assumed the situation where you must start from scratch to build interest in a problem in order to secure cooperation in acting upon it. However, it is far easier to get problems solved in an organization where the interest already exists—where there is a climate that makes problem-solving an accepted way of doing business. Building such a climate should be a full-time concern for the manager who wants to make his own life easier over the long pull.

There are several steps you can take to help build this climate. The first one is to demonstrate your own receptiveness to ideas and suggestions against existing problems. Some executives regularly schedule meetings to talk over their problems with subordinates. This is done in an atmosphere conducive to encouraging subordinates to make suggestions—and with some demonstration that the suggestions are being listened to. Along with the communication of problems, of course, should go some communication of rewards, if any, for solutions. If the reward is psychic rather than monetary, this requires only that the executive first think through which emotional appeal is apt to gain the greatest amount of interest from his listeners, and then plan his presentation of the problem in those terms.

Of course many of the problems an executive faces must be communicated individually to persons who will be expected to contribute on them. But individually or collectively, there are some further guides in presenting your problems to others in order to take maximum advantage of what interest they will give you.

The first is be patient. It is good principle to assume that others may not react to a new problem with the same enthusiasm and initial understanding that you yourself have. If they seem slow in grasping the problem, or the opportunity, hold back on your haste in either condemning them or rejecting them as the instrument of solution. Ask yourself first if you have really explained the problem in an understandable way. Did you state it clearly, for example?—or did you indulge yourself in the vanity of using the language of the problem that someone new to it would not understand? Did you assume familiarity with the problem situation that could not realistically be expected to exist? Or did you misjudge your man in terms of what would motivate him to take an interest in your problem? Too often, in the hurry to "get on with it," an executive can commit all these errors in presenting a problem to a subordinate, and then blame the subordinate when he fails to grasp the problem and to make progress against it.

Another principle of maintaining interest in solving problems is that once you have put a man on a problem, give him the freedom to go at it in his own way. One instructor in the command department, U.S. Naval Academy, covers this aspect of leadership this way:

"Nothing destroys a young officer's initiative more quickly than a senior who will not put a problem into his hands without constantly instructing and advising while the subordinate is trying to solve it. Successfully completed staff work," he continues, "requires the senior to tell the subordinate what the problem is, without telling him how to solve it; provide the subordinate a general statement of organizational policies in the premise; and schedule a reasonable deadline for completion." And he concludes, "In the interim, it is the senior's implicit duty to leave the subordinate to his own devices, dismissing the problem until the solution is returned for approval at the time specified."

This does not mean, however, that a superior cannot keep in touch with work in progress on a problem. One of the initial statements of policy provided the subordinate should cover the frequency of reporting expected and/or the types of developments which call for immediate notification of the superior.

In summary, we can say that the executive who wants to get problems solved faster, more creatively, and more productively, will study the problem in order to find the basic appeals that will motivate his people to take the highest degree of interest in it. But this must be done sincerely and honestly, with complete understanding of both the people and the problem.

Basically, human nature is skeptical enough to know

when it is being presented with an "opportunity" that is not really an opportunity. And, while it is both possible and morally acceptable for a manager to attempt to enlist a subordinate's emotional responses to capture his interest in solving a problem, it is dangerous for that manager to attempt to do this on an unsound basis.

The nature of the spur should be in keeping with the nature of the problem to be solved. Finding a correlation or natural linkup of the two may require a certain amount of analysis, or even unexpected ingenuity. But these are the kinds of thinking any company has a right to expect of its managers. They are, in fact, the kinds of problems the manager should be expected to solve as his own responsibility.

*The manager must know himself in order to
be able to maximize his own capabilities, to
make the most of his own strengths, and to
develop methods to compensate for his
weaker qualities.*

13

Measure Your
Own Performance

One of the most difficult things for anyone to do —be he manager, college professor, minister, or mind reader —is to take a good hard look at himself in his job. In fact, no matter how objective a man may be in other situations, it is practically impossible for the average person to be objective about himself.

Furthermore, every manager today is subjected to almost limitless amounts of advice on what it takes to be a good boss. He often finds, therefore, some difficulty in selecting a particular set of standards against which to measure his own skills as a practical manager.

But when all the verbiage is cleared away, when all the conflicting advice and opinions have been reconciled, the standards for a good boss usually net down to *four*. The good boss knows

His people
Their working conditions
His organization
His own responsibilities

The questions in this chapter will help you appraise your own strengths and weaknesses within these four critical areas.

How well do you know your people?

Professor Leo B. Moore, School of Industrial Management, M.I.T., says, "The executive must realize and believe that 'Without the people, I don't operate.'" Therefore, the first questions any boss should ask himself concern his relationships with others.

Are you delegating as much as you should? The textbooks say that delegating is a matter of organization and communications. But as we have seen, it is more—it is the real key to survival for a boss. The boss's job is to get things done —but not to do them all himself. If he is to grow, personally, he must have time for thinking and planning for the orderly growth of his company. If he finds himself so saddled with details, unfinished tasks, and "low-level" working arrangements that he has no time to think, he cannot do what he is paid to do.

Is your delegation as complete as it should be? Or can't you quite resist keeping that one little string tied to the authority you have ostensibly delegated to do a job? Good management—meaning, in this instance, good delegation —basically consists of finding the right man to do a job for you. When you think you have found him, give him every opportunity and freedom to prove himself until he satisfies you, or proves himself incapable of handling the responsibility. But let him run his own show and make his own mistakes. Or, if you insist on keeping your finger in the pie to some extent, don't try to kid either the man or yourself into thinking that you are giving him a completely free hand. You aren't.

How often are you interrupted with a new idea? The good boss welcomes the ideas of others. He may also, on occasion, plant his own ideas in the minds of others and compliment them on their ingenuity. It's what Dr. G. Herbert True terms your D.I.I.Q.—meaning, daily idea interruption quotient. If you are frequently interrupted by your workers with new suggestions or ideas for your consideration, chances are your quotient is high. On the other hand, if you seldom receive suggestions for new and better ways of doing things, better look at your habits and practices in the reception of new ideas.

Are your people with growth potential placed where they have the best potential to grow? It is not enough today just to find people with all the needed capabilities to do the job you hired them to do, and then leave them alone to do it. There are just too many better jobs going begging for people to fill them. Therefore, a manager will try to help his people "maximize their maximums" by giving them every opportunity to grow above their present capabilities. No workers should ever have to come to you to ask for more work or more responsibility. No worker should ever feel he has to quit you and go some place else for more opportunity. If these things happen, you have been missing the clues that point to a man with growth potential who can also help your company grow.

Do your workers really know what they are trying to accomplish? Do you explain to key subordinates the whys behind any particular task they are asked to do? Do they know exactly what final result you want to accomplish and understand the proposed method of accomplishment? Furthermore, do you personally spend time making sure that the "whys" have been passed down to the people under them? By presenting jobs or work assignments to others in terms of the desired accomplishment, the boss fulfills his key responsibility of planning the policy and strategy, but leaves the tactics up to the people who are charged with the doing. Much confusion and wheel spinning will be saved if the boss also presents any necessary "whys" with the task.

How often do you contact each individual member of your own group? Any good manager, of course, maintains an open door policy for anyone who has cause—real or imagined—to see him. Furthermore, he makes sure that the mind beyond the door is also open. But it is also important that the executive initiate some communications himself. He should build a working knowledge of his immediate subordinates through regular personal contact. In smaller working groups, he should know all his workers' names, and be able to address them by name; he must be familiar with their personality characteristics and capabilities in order to direct their efforts most effectively. And only by actual first-hand knowledge of his workers can a boss check on those important intangibles of morale and attitude that so strongly affect the success or failure of a business operation.

Do you consider the "chemistry" of people? People put in contact with one another tend to react like chemicals. The boss is the chemist who must make sure that the reactions obtained by mixtures of personalities will be to the good of the business. This is more than just preventing explosions. It demands enough skill and forethought to be able to combine individual characters, with all their differences of backgrounds, educations, environmental upbringings, and experiences in a dependable, useful, and profitable way. In your regular relationships and work assignments, you, as the boss, cannot afford to like people or dislike them on the basis of their personal chemical attributes, any more than a chemist can let himself be influenced by the odor or color of certain chemicals. The job is to make these differences in human chemical characteristics work to the best advantage of what you are trying to accomplish.

Do you have any individual attitude problems? The attitude of a worker depends, primarily, on his reaction to the particular spirit of a work group, and his own feelings of adequacy or proficiency in his job. A highly proficient workman will, if he is being challenged to his capacity, have a positive, progressive attitude—one that bespeaks pride toward his work. A man insufficiently trained, or lacking the confidence that comes from understanding what is expected of him, may show it with an outwardly negative attitude. On the other hand, if everyone in your whole group or department seems to lack a positive attitude, you may have to look beyond the group to possible external causes, such as your company's communications program, wage levels, general personnel policies, or working conditions, in order to diagnose it. In the case of either the individual or the group problem, however, you, as the boss, must assume the responsibility for clearing it up. Your unit personality is your responsibility, and you are the person to apply the leadership to make it a positive one.

How are working conditions?

Few managers will deny the advantages of an efficient, productive plant layout, or of using the latest available types of production equipment. By the same token, poor or substandard working facilities or atmospheres can have an adverse effect on morale and spirit.

Do you show a personal interest in working conditions? Your interest should extend to such features as the cleanliness and sanitation of the environment, the quality of housekeeping that may indicate workers' attitudes, and the neatness and cleanliness of the workers themselves—all subject, naturally, to the limitations of the type of work being done. A manager who interests himself in the way his workers live while under his direction will usually find it repaid in confidence, respect, and willingness to cooperate far beyond that called for by the paycheck only.

How long since you've conducted a safety review? If your responsibility includes supervising a hazardous operation, safety is one item you cannot neglect. You must give frequent and personal and visible attention to the various activities related to a safety program, particularly those related to the safety of the personnel. But even in less hazardous businesses, such as retailing, safety checks are important. It makes no difference whether a broken leg is caused by a piece of heavy machinery or a slip on a poorly lighted staircase—the leg is still broken, and worker morale is affected.

Make safety checks an important part of your regular review of working conditions.

How do your workers feel about their working conditions? It would be a mistake, of course, to depend entirely upon worker opinions in estimating the quality of working conditions simply because you will never be able to please everyone without exception. On the other hand, workers appreciate being asked about such things, and have, on occasion, been known to come up with concrete suggestions that had been missed by the full-time "experts" in efficiency and safety. Furthermore, if you form the habit of listening to what your people mean, as opposed to what they say, you will be able to determine much about their mental attitudes both toward their jobs and the company.

How does your organization fit in?

Any department, section, division, or other standard breakdown of the company as a whole, represents an organization that must be integrated into the larger operation in an effective, efficient way. This, of course, is the responsibility of the boss of that particular subgroup, and this raises questions which you should ask yourself about the organization under your direction, whatever size it may be.

How well does your group understand their role in the overall company activities? Among the ways you can evaluate this is by noting any expressions (or lack of them) from workers showing enthusiasm and pride in what they are doing, or what the department as a whole has managed to accomplish. You can also check your effectiveness rating by finding out what kind of a reputation your group has among other company units. Other readily observable indications are the willingness workers have to pitch in and help one another, the knowledge they have of what goes on in other departments around them, and what they know of what happens both before and after their own jobs. One of the best ways of raising the "organizational consciousness" of individual workers is to make sure that new help receive a full orientation and indoctrination upon joining your group. The worker who knows why he is doing a job usually does it better.

How is your group's general morale today? Organizational morale does not remain constant, but is in a continual state of change. The day-to-day morale of your group will show a direct relationship with the day-to-day efficiency. Therefore, regular evaluation will serve to give you an index for predicting organizational efficiency. Specific indicators to take note of include job proficiency of individuals; general courtesy and personal hygiene; care of equipment and supplies; responses to orders or suggestions; attendance at training sessions; number of rumors; quarrels and feuds among workers; absenteeism; waste and reject ratios. In studying any of these, the day-to-day indications are not so important as any sudden or unexplained changes that might point up a morale problem in the making.

What do you personally contribute to morale? Because the efficiency and productivity of a group is so closely tied to morale, it behooves every manager to make sure his own contributions are both positive and constructive. For example, a biographer of the aeronautical designer, Igor Sikorsky, reports that Sikorsky never gave an order. "If you don't mind," he would say; or "If this suggestion is not in conflict with your own engineering principles..." But so great was Sikorsky's prestige and capability for leadership that his proposal became an order. And if a man came to him with a suggestion, he would say, "Excellent! Now let's work it out this way..." and, busily sketching, he would make radical changes. When the part got into production, it was often Sikorsky's design, but the employee believed it was his. Consequently, morale in Sikorsky's work groups was always high and the general outlook for success was always highly optimistic.

How much of your time do you spend supervising training? The proficiency of your group as a whole depends upon the sum of proficiencies of the individuals. The proficiency and effectiveness of any individual depends to a great extent upon the thoroughness of his training. Therefore close interest in, and supervision of, any training activities within your department should occupy a significant portion of your time and attention. You will get proficiency only when you set high standards and insist they be met. Among the standards to use in judging efficiency and effectiveness are, of course, the results your organization can achieve under any conditions of operation: willing acceptance and discharge of responsibilities by your immediate subordinates; a businesslike attitude in the department or unit; promptness and accuracy in communicating instructions and information; and promptness and accuracy in any feedback to you of information that can only come from bottom to top.

What are your responsibilities?

It is too broad a generalization to say the boss is responsible for everything that goes on in his department, but there is no denying that he must take the final responsibility for the results his department achieves. But, as mentioned in the first chapter, results are a total thing. You can get results in an efficient way, or show a profit, or contribute to the long-term progress and growth of the company. And, of course, you can produce results in such a way that the people you have used to get them don't all apply for transfers to another department or leave to join another company. Therefore, achieving results is a many sided and often complex challenge.

Are your personal habits on the job above reproach? The French psychologist Gabriel Tarde claims that people react to each other mainly by conscious or unconscious imitation. This suggests that a boss must always be alert to the necessity for keeping his personal conduct on the highest level, if only to prevent imitation of his bad habits on the part of subordinates. Certainly, it does not take much observation of various work groups to see the reflection of the man-in-charge among his immediate subordinates. Let a boss be positive, cheerful, and optimistic come what may, and chances are the same "go-go-go" attitude will be reflected throughout his group. Let the boss be negative, seclusive, and suspicious, and the group personality will be most disagreeably the same way.

Have you determined whom your successor should be? More than one small company has foundered and failed because of the failure of the top man to provide for and train his successor in the company. In this respect, top management's greatest responsibility may well be to train its succession. And it is undoubtedly true that the fastest way to rise in a big company is not to step on the people under you, but to give them freedom to grow and the credit for accomplishment. The boss who does this can count on the reciprocity of his people in pushing him up in the company. In any case, every boss should know who his most likely successor should be in the event of a promotion for himself. This means, also, that he be willing to indoctrinate and train the successor so that, should promotion beckon for the boss, he will not be held back himself waiting for a successor to be trained to take over his present job.

Have you learned the principle of positive discipline? Discipline is usually thought of in its narrowest sense, as a punishment for wrongdoing. But in the broader sense, discipline is that attitude or force in an individual or group that insures prompt carrying out of orders and the initiation of proper action in the absence of orders. The advantage of the positive approach to discipline is that it instills a helpful, potent spirit into an organization that will build group cohesion and motivate the individuals. For the boss, this again makes it mandatory that he demonstrate self-discipline in his own conduct and by his own example. He must set his own performance standards high and live up to them. Discipline, in the positive sense, is the result of mutual confidence and understanding between a leader and his followers.

Do you know how to administer corrective discipline? If the boss must be oriented toward action and results, then there are times when he must be a disciplinarian, no matter how much he may personally dislike the chore. When it is necessary to administer discipline, in any of its various administrative forms, the prime rule, of course, is that you be fair, consistent, prompt, and impersonal. One major caution in deciding the need for disciplinary action comes from George Bernard Shaw in his observation that "reasonable people adapt themselves to the world; unreasonable people adapt the world to them. All progress is made by unreasonable people." It can be a mistake to jump too hastily to the conclusion that a person who breaks the rules merits immediate discipline. It may be that he has found a better way than that called for in the rules. Nonconformists can be valuable to your progress. Discipline them with caution.

How many of your subordinates are working on self-improvement programs? Any person who manages people is judged by the people he develops. Development for a subordinate should usually take two forms: training, by which he learns his job and operation in the company scheme of things, and, for the more ambitious workers, self-development programs that are either suggested or initiated by the man's supervisor or boss. Nearly every worker has the capacity for some degree of self-improvement on his job that will make him a more valuable asset to the company. And, in the long run, it is usually cheaper to upgrade the talent you have than to buy it on the open market. Therefore, it is the boss's responsibility to appraise his people periodically and suggest ways and means for them to speed their personal growth and advancement.

How flexible is your training program? Although every worker has some capacity to grow in his job, no two workers have the same ultimate capacity nor do they grow at the same rate. Therefore, a good boss uses his knowledge of his people to pace their training and development to their individual speeds of progress. Furthermore, the training or development program must take into account the individual capabilities and aptitudes of the worker on the program. Crawford H. Greenewalt, while president of E. I. du Pont de Nemours & Co., said in a lecture at Columbia University: "The organization is in trouble when success causes it to be so enraptured with its accomplishments that it is moved, like Narcissus, to fashion everything to its own image.... Too much codification in our training procedures can result in perpetuating a facsimile and freezing rigid patterns of thought. Thorough training is obviously a necessity, but it must always be remembered that organizations do not make men—it is men who make organizations; it is what they bring with them in the way of character and adaptability and fresh ideas that enriches the organizational blood stream and insures corporate longevity."

How long since you have given a personal progress report to each of your men? It is, as we have said, the boss's responsibility to encourage individual development by suggesting educational opportunities to his men and supporting educational and training programs when offered by the company. But more than this, the boss should remember that all men want to know how well they have done, and what will be expected of them in the future. The individual who is well informed as to his situation and his future opportunities is more effective than one kept in the dark. Keeping a man informed, furthermore, is a form of individual recognition that promotes initiative and improves morale.

Can your people judge their own ideas? It is one thing to be open-minded and receptive to new ideas if you are the boss. But all ideas are not good, and your workers should not waste your time with minor whims that have no possibility of even a long-range development (even though, if they present such ideas, you, the boss, still have to listen to them!). A good idea has to be both usable, or capable of being made so, and a definite change for the better. If your workers consistently ignore these criteria, it may point up a deficiency in the training program. There may be too much emphasis on a specific way to accomplish something, with a lack of indoctrination into principles. True learning and insight come from a thorough grasp of basic principles, and the use of principles enables a person to solve new problems and judge new ideas for value almost instinctively and immediately.

Do you pass along credit for the originator with every new idea? It is not very intelligent for anyone to assume the credit for the work of others. As the boss, it is your job and prime responsibility to produce results for the company. Therefore, you will automatically receive credit anyway. It is only smart operating for the boss to give credit to the man who has earned it, whether for a new idea or for surpassing a production standard.

How do you coach, from the backfield or the sidelines? It is always a temptation, when you watch a subordinate struggling to solve a problem to which you know the answers, to jump into the play yourself and get the ball moving again. But, by so doing, you not only deprive the man of the opportunity to make his own contribution to the problem solution, you also eliminate any opportunity for him to find a better way of handling the job than you yourself might have among your answers. Furthermore, it is an infringement on the delegation you have made. So the wise boss will, no matter how much it hurts, content himself with coaching in an exploratory manner by suggesting avenues of inquiry and lines of endeavor as possibilities.

Now, how good a boss are you?

Every manager or potential manager or would-be manager must start with what he has: himself. And he must build on that as well as he is able. And he must do it himself. A company can give any man the title of "manager," but only the man can make himself into one.

14

Improving Your Management Skills Starts with You

In commenting on current interest in increasing the supply of executive talent and leadership for American business, William M. Allen, president of the Boeing Company, said, "I would submit that with respect to both leadership and talent, our need is not necessarily for more, but for better use of what we have."

Mr. Allen also made the point that "If you are setting out to improve the effectiveness of management talent, I am doubtful that the existence of a formal program of development and training alone will be sufficient."

The purpose of this chapter is to review some of the steps the manager himself must personally take if he wants to become better at his job—the things that go beyond formal development programs and basic principles and without which even the best of programs and principles cannot succeed in developing an executive. These steps involve you, your attitudes, and your actions. You won't need anyone else's approval or cooperation to put them into practice, and the only person you need communicate them to is always available.

Face it: Only you can make yourself a better manager

Training, development programs, and continued study definitely do have a place in the making of a manager. Through making it possible to share in the experiences of others, they can add to knowledge. By providing distilled principles of action, they give guidance. Through the stimulation of new intellectual exposures, they provide a necessary background of confidence that is of inestimable value to the man with the responsibility for making decisions. But academic study can go only so far. One instructor of a creative management course makes this point strongly to his students in the last session. "Don't consider your course completion Certificates to mean you are 'Graduate Creative Thinkers,' " he warns. "Accept them; keep them; display them prominently some place where you will see them every day. But use them as reminders that you have invested some time, energy, and mental anguish to complete this course as a beginning to what is now expected of you. But from here on out, it is up to you whether or not you will make this course pay off for yourself and your company."

And this, of course, is the crux of management development of any kind. All personal development is just that —personal. As Emerson put it, "Self-trust is the first secret of success." It is up to the manager to trust his own capabilities to make a success of the training he has been given and to develop the attitudes and experience that must be truly self-developed because they cannot be taught.

Realize that you are you—and make the most of it

One of the most common misconceptions about being an executive in any organization is that there is some mystical pattern or mold that the aspiring manager should cast himself in if he wants to make the grade. And this is certainly the first attitude that an aspirant should divest himself of. You cannot make the most of your own inborn talents if you try to develop along the lines of any set or ideal or specified pattern of personality characteristics, because the reality of the situation is that there are no set patterns for success.

Consider the most common example of "regimented personalities": the military. Certainly if any group, as a group, has an image of inflexible sameness, it is a military organization. Yet in *The Professional Soldier,* Morris Janowitz points out that most distinguished commanders were men who deviated from the image. General MacArthur, for example, is cited as having a "career based on a flouting of authority." The Marine Corps' General Holland Smith is quoted in his own description of himself: "I was a bad boy. I always have been a bad boy in interservice arguments and I often am amazed that I lasted so long...." And the description by Marquis Childs of Dwight Eisenhower may come as a shock to anyone whose image of him is that of the conservative he became in later years. As a West Point cadet, according to Childs, "Eisenhower was a roughneck. He broke the rules just as often as he dared. Law abiding classmates were shocked at his daring.... His conduct was that of the tough boy from the wrong side of the tracks, defying the code, and yet managing by his resourcefulness to live with it."

Certainly if such individualistic personalities can succeed in a military organization, they should also do well in even the most image-conscious business and commercial enterprises.

One industrialist who expressed himself on this point is

Alfred C. Fuller, founder of the Fuller Brush Company. "Of the first two hundred men who achieved executive position in the Fuller Brush Company," he relates, "only three had previously earned as much as fifty dollars a week in other employment. They were without exception little men of no previous attainment, or inadequate background, and almost no training for their jobs. Neither they nor I could 'think big'; we just knew how to work hard."

Albert Einstein, noted for his individualism, stressed his feelings of the importance of individuality just before he died with his statement that one of the few things he felt sure of is that no person is just like any other person—"the individual is unique."

The late Moorhead Wright, of the General Electric Company, not only supported the feeling that the best service a company can give its managers is to allow them to be their own men, but also raised some interesting questions regarding theoretical images for managers:

"If you are going to work toward any sort of ideal 'personality pattern,'" he asked, "what, in the face of such a pattern, are you going to say to the managers now in place? Shall we say that they must conform to this ideal pattern or be fired? How," he continued, "do we account for the fact that we now have some managers—good managers—who are tough and rugged personalities, others who are quiet and thoughtful men, others who are aggressive-salesmen types, and others just as widely assorted—all good managers? The truth is," he concludes, "there just isn't any standard pattern of personality traits that make a good manager."

Go after experience right where you are

A research project in General Electric involved interviews with 300 men who had reached positions where they had managerial responsibilities. An outside research group was utilized, and individuals were guaranteed anonymity. In response to the question "What do you consider the thing that was most important in your development?" 90 per cent of the managers replied that it was the day-to-day work they were involved in. Only 10 per cent attributed major developmental importance to educational background, special courses, job rotation, etc. The outstanding factors were the manner in which the man himself was managed in his daily work, the climate in which he worked, and his relationships with others—particularly his immediate managers.

Amron H. Katz, in commenting on the value of his own past experience as a designer as a guide to the work he is now doing in aeronautical engineering, states the case this way: "Experience is not always a good teacher, nor is past experience necessarily and universally relevant to the future. On the other hand, it would indeed be strange if, after two decades of studies, experiments, and participation with the military in design, test, evaluation, and use of equipment in the air as well as on the ground, in observations on the use of equipment in the field, under a full spectrum of conditions from primitive to plush—if at the end of all this I didn't have some firmly held views on what kind of developments are likely to succeed, what kind of developments are likely to fail—and why."

George Bunker, chairman and chief executive officer of the Martin Company, pointed up one of the real values of first-hand experience in commenting on reorganizations following the troubles that company had in its development work on the Titan missile: "If you burn your fingers lighting a match," he said, "you're going to be more careful next time."

And Joyce Clyde Hall, founder and president of Hallmark Greeting Cards, is famous for his reliance on what he calls "the vapor of experience" in reaching his decisions.

The prime cautionary note to be sounded regarding the principle of going after new experience in your present job is that you must be sure your assigned work is being done. Many eager junior executives realize that even limited management authority brings opportunities to develop themselves through sharing different experiences, but they then make the mistake of working so hard to broaden their horizons that they forget to cover the daily bases they are paid to cover. So while your present job offers you the base for future growth, you probably won't prosper to any great extent if the company's work that is assigned to you isn't being done.

But opportunities to take on new responsibilities and gain the experience that comes from solving the problems connected with them are all around any person in an executive job. They exist in the improved utilization of people; better control of dollars; more efficient and effective use of time; and maximum utilization of company facilities. Few companies, or even divisions, departments, or sections of companies can claim that they are doing the absolute best that can be expected in all of these areas, and anyone looking for opportunities will find plenty of them without having to carry the search very far.

Help your people grow

Industrialist Henry Kaiser states, "I make progress by having people around me who are smarter than I am—and listening to them. And I assume that everyone is smarter about something than I am."

This is really the secret of effective development and maximum utilization of subordinates' talents: determine what the best qualities are of each of your people, and then give them the opportunities to maximize those qualities for the benefit of the company. This means, of course, that everyone in an organization will then have opportunities to grow. This requires a consciousness by the executive of the potential that lies within every man to develop new capabilities and capacities when the climate is right.

One company that makes a deliberate policy of allowing their people to maximize whatever potentials they may have as individuals is Aerojet-General Corporation. Although called highly unorthodox for their organization and operating methods, the company has achieved some startling successes in the highly competitive aerospace industry by following such far-out procedures as allowing the scientists who develop new devices to trot out and attempt to sell them to prospective customers themselves. So far the policy has paid off with more successes than failures, and has come to be the way things are expected to happen all through the company.

Furthermore, no executive can expect subordinates to be ready to take over new responsibilities as suddenly as can be demanded in a situation of rapid growth or unexpected emergency if those subordinates have not previously had the opportunity to practice handling responsibilities on a smaller scale and under noncritical conditions. Even if we were to discount by 50 per cent the predictions of future shortages in executive talent to be available for business, the importance of developing new talents through offering the opportunities to juniors to grow is still an apparent one. As the late J. H. Kindelberger, former chairman of North American Aviation, once said, "Nobody ever pulled a rabbit out of a hat without carefully putting it there in the first place."

The kind of delegation that builds the character of the subordinate, and equips him with the confidence to step out and achieve, is masterfully described by General Matthew B. Ridgway in his biography, *Soldier*. He tells of being assigned the command of the Eighth Army in Korea at the time when the situation was far from encouraging for the UN forces.

"At nine," recalls General Ridgway, "I saw General Mac-Arthur. In a masterful briefing, he covered all the points I had in mind to ask him. As I rose to go, I asked one question. 'General,' I said, 'If I get over there and find the situation warrants it, do I have your permission to attack?'"

"A broad grin broke out on the old gentleman's face. 'Do what you think best, Matt,' he said, 'The Eighth Army is yours.'

"That," says Ridgway, "is the sort of orders that puts heart into a soldier."

An example of a similar order in business is one credited to Donald Power, chairman and chief executive of General Telephone & Electronics Corporation. In instructing a newly promoted head of one of the company's areas, he is reported to have said, "I want only three things: high morale, good earnings, and good public relations. If you achieve these, you don't have to bother to send me any other reports."

Mr. Power thereby demonstrated another cardinal principle of good delegation: he knew what he wanted and was able to communicate it.

Aim for professionalism

"I like pros," said one manager. "I like to listen to them: watch them in action; work with them; know I have one on the job when there is a major commitment to be met. I don't care how snobbish it sounds, I always prefer to deal with a pro."

You will, of course, find pros in other than management jobs, too: the salesman who never gets flustered or never makes a mistake, no matter how difficult the customer makes the interview.

Or the soft-talking engineer who quietly moves in on a test bench where an instrument that is supposed to take an

American to the moon and back is being tested—and not working. This pro listens to all the explanations of why it won't work and then softly asks the one question no one else had thought of asking—and gets the project moving again.

What's more, it isn't just in business that you can find the pros: you'll see waitresses in restaurants who seem able to handle twice the number of customers with half the effort of the other girls on the floor; bus drivers who never get rattled in the heaviest rush-hour traffic, but manage with quiet good humor to keep both their passengers at ease and their tightly drawn schedules; and shoe shine boys who always take the time to give that extra slap of the cloth that puts the highest gloss on the leather—and who always say "thank you" with a smile that says they mean it.

Certainly being a professional in a job is more than just a matter of being paid for it. There are people in jobs they are paid for doing who never seem to shine as brightly as others in similar positions. Professionalism is more a matter of the attitudes that manifest themselves in a man's general approach to his work.

One such characteristic is often the man's willingness to stick his neck out to a greater degree than his colleagues when a new proposition is presented. As Admiral Rickover states: "The first thing a man has to do is to realize that he is going to get his head chopped off ultimately. If he has that feeling, perhaps he can accomplish something."

Another characteristic of the pro is his complete mastery of his job, no matter how complex the problem. Ben Mills, an associate of Robert McNamara in his Ford Motor Company days, tells of McNamara's intellectual abilities in problem solving sessions. After listening to arguments and propositions from his staff on highly complex problems, McNamara would then take over. "It was incredible," says Mills. "He would rattle off a dozen or more points, often without having taken any notes. If you challenged him, he was likely to defeat you with figures and judgments you yourself had given him several months earlier. It takes a certain amount of genius to be able to absorb and make sense of tough problems as quickly as Bob does. But, more than that, it takes a lot of intense study, a lot of damned hard work."

Another easily observed quality in the real professional is his personal sense of responsibility. The real pro seldom waits for problems to come to him—he goes out looking for problems, and when he finds one he can get his teeth into, he makes it his own personal problem and doesn't sit or quit until that problem has been licked. Frank Fisher, of the management consulting firm of Cresap, McCormick, and Paget, cites the opposite of this attitude as the symptom of a "stale climate" in a company. In the stale climate organization, according to Fisher, executives tend to be acquiescent —they don't develop strong feelings about anything and never bother to disagree over issues. Such men, he points out, tend to play "follow the leader"; they lack a feeling of urgency and therefore tend to postpone decisions. And this, indicates Fisher, is when the businesses begin to run down.

Still another manifestation of the sense of responsibility that makes a pro is when the man realizes he is living in a world greater than just his job. Charles Percy, president of Bell & Howell, may typify the new breed of executive with a sense of both national and international responsibilities in addition to his duties to his company. He is a member of the board of the University of Chicago; chairman of the Ford Foundation's Fund for Adult Education; and chairman of the Republican Party's Policy Committee on Programs and Progress. Says Percy, "If all of us in industry learned better the world in which we live, we'd all be better individuals."

Another readily observable characteristic of a pro is that he goes at his work with the realization that temperament is never a substitute for ability—he knows that it is always better to *be* right than to sound right. He measures his own performance by his own standards—and these are usually higher than anyone else would dream of setting for him. Finally, it is never an accident, or a lucky break, when a pro does an outstanding job. He planned it that way, and wouldn't let it happen otherwise.

Guard your moral values

Few men in any field ever reach the ultimate top without a strong sense of moral values. The occasional man who does gain a position of prestige or power with a character not completely honest will soon be uncovered for the weakness. Power or authority demands integrity of the highest type, for without it the occupant of the position will sooner or later give in to the temptation to abuse his authority. And even in lesser positions, a strong and sincere sense of morality is a requisite for winning and holding the respect and confidence of others in the face of the everyday temptations to deal and contrive as being easier alternatives to thinking and planning.

To say that a man can be a little dishonest in business is comparable to saying that a woman can be a little bit pregnant. A man is either honest or he is not; he either has integrity or he does not. And it is not required that he be a psalm-singing Bible thumper for him to be a moralist. As a matter of fact, unless he does have true and deep religious convictions, for him to adopt a superreligious pose merely for the sake of appearances would indicate a lack of integrity.

The practice of honesty has, in many industries, become a way of life—as it should for all businesses. Advertising agencies, for example, despite all the public abuse that is occasionally heaped upon them by critics of one sort or another, are noted for the "word is his bond" nature of their relationships with media representatives and suppliers. An agency executive will bargain like a longshoreman's union chieftain to get favorable arrangements for his clients, and may get into bitter and even recriminatory arguments with the media representative or supplier of the moment. But once agreement is reached, everyone knows that the contract can follow whenever it is convenient. Its main purpose will be a record of the transaction.

Corporate reputations for honesty often pay off in dramatic ways. Donald Douglas built such a reputation for his aircraft company and worked to preserve it despite the strongest temptations. One such was deliberately put in his way by Captain Eddie Rickenbacker at the time Douglas was competing against Boeing to sell Eastern Airlines its first big jets. During the negotiations, Rickenbacker is said to have told Douglas that his specifications and offers for the DC-8 were close to Boeing on everything but noise suppression. He then gave Douglas one last chance to out-promise Boeing on this feature.

After consulting with his engineers, Douglas reported back to Rickenbacker with the news that he did not feel he could make the promise. Rickenbacker is said to have replied, "I know you can't. I wanted to see if you were still honest. You just got yourself an order for $165 million. Now go home and silence those damn jets!"

Another Douglas, Senator Paul, demonstrates the force of integrity against the pressures of group conformity. Senator Douglas has the reputation of always walking alone, often in the face of what is usually referred to as party discipline. He explains his policy in easily understood terms: "One rule I make," he says, "is that if procedure does not vitally affect substance, I will follow my party on procedural grounds. But when substance is involved, I will follow my conscience."

A demonstration of reliance on personal integrity in dealings with others was given by Edgar Kaiser in settling with the United Steelworkers in the face of solid industry opposition to settlement. Kaiser, relying on his own judgment of the situation, explained his decision: "We do not believe it's right to put people back to work under a court injunction," he said. "When you force things upon human beings, you simply make more trouble for yourself in the long run. We think a showdown with labor, an attempt to turn the clock back, will merely result in more government control."

Such views are becoming more and more recognized as the hallmarks of enlightened management today. The blinding glare of publicity resulting from a well-intentioned, if somewhat overzealous, government policy of suspecting everything and everyone in business, is serving the purpose of lighting up the shadows where the big-riggers, the over-friendly noncompeting competitors, and the influence peddlers once did their business. And the only men who will survive with the freedom to pursue truly free enterprise are those whose moral standards are, like Caesar's wife, above suspicion.

To sum up, then, it is apparent that individual improvement must be largely an individual matter. While outside-induced education and academic experience do have much to offer a manager for his own personal development, only the man himself can supply or develop the inner qualities that transcend methods, techniques, procedures, and systems. You start where you are with what you have to work with now and build on it.

And only you can make yourself a better manager.

Index

235

Catalog

If you are interested in a list of fine Paperback
books, covering a wide range of subjects
and interests, send your name and address,
requesting your free catalog, to:

McGraw-Hill Paperbacks
1221 Avenue of Americas
New York, N.Y. 10020